LUNCH WITH JOE

LUNCH WITH JOE

Peter Legge
with
Tashon Ziara

Eaglet Publishing

Eaglet Publishing
Peter Legge Management Co. Ltd.
4th Floor, 4180 Lougheed Highway
Burnaby, British Columbia, V5C 6A7, Canada
Tel. (604) 299-7311 Fax (604) 299-9188

Library and Archives Canada Cataloguing in Publication

Legge, Peter, 1942-
Lunch with Joe / Peter Legge with, Tashon Ziara.
ISBN 978-0-9878194-1-3

1. Segal, Joe. 2. Businessmen--British Columbia--Vancouver--Biography. 3. Success in business. I. Title.

FC3830.1.S44L44 2013 971.1'3305092 C2013-901299-0
First Printing
Jacket design by Catherine Mullaly; cover photo by Paul Joseph; electronic imaging by Debbie Craig;
Typeset by Ina Bowerbank
Edited by Kim Mah
Printed and bound in Canada by Friesens

Other Books by the Author

How to Soar With the Eagles

You Can If You Believe You Can

It Begins With a Dream

If Only I'd Said That

If Only I'd Said That: Volume II

If Only I'd Said That: Volume III

If Only I'd Said That: Volume IV

If Only I'd Said That: Volume V

If Only I'd Said That: Volume VI

Who Dares Wins

The Runway of Life

Make Your Life a Masterpiece

The Power of Tact

The Power to Soar Higher

The Power of a Dream

365 Days of Insights

Booklets

97 Tips on How to Do Business in Tough Times

97 Tips on Customer Service

97 Tips on How to Jumpstart Your Career

CD

The Runway of Life

To Joe and Rosalie Segal

You are valued friends and a true inspiration

TABLE OF CONTENTS

INTRODUCTION

Most philanthropic humans are the kindest people you could ever meet or they are the smartest people you've ever met. Normally, those two don't usually go together, but when I think of Joe Segal, the words kind, compassionate, smart and humble come to mind. Joe has been a great friend and supporter of my foundation for many years. When I see Joe, he puts a smile on my face, he lights up a room when he enters . . . if there were more people in this world like Joe and Rosalie, the world would be a better place!

David Foster, O.C., O.B.C.

FOREWORD

When my dear friend Peter Legge mused about a book celebrating my father's accomplishments, I naively asked if it could be ready by June 2013. To benefit Coast Mental Health, the Vancouver Board of Trade was planning a gala, *Joe Segal: an Extraordinary Life*; a book honouring my father would be a touching addition to the evening. Peter, a well-seasoned author and publisher, regretfully said the timeline was not possible. "Unless . . . " he began, and with that, the idea for this book was born. *Lunch With Joe* is a collection of recollections, written by the very people who met him for lunch at the Four Seasons Vancouver, to talk, think and seek guidance. Their names are too many to list here, but to all I offer my deepest gratitude.

Human relationships, and how we sustain them, are at the very core of my father's creed. His ability to reach out to people, his passion to help them and his willingness to do what is difficult has endeared him to so many. On the following pages are vignettes from a varied cast of characters: business titans and politicians, rabbis and priests, colleagues and representatives of those in need. Each story is unique, yet all carry a unifying theme: Joe Segal helped them to be a better person.

To my father I say that in everything I do, I carry the lessons you have modelled throughout your life. I never tire of telling people that you taught me much more than "what to do"; you taught me "the way to do it." That fair play and a sense of responsibility make up the foundation to a meaningful life. And that, in and of itself, money will not give us the feeling we are all looking for; it is what we do with it that counts. My own community work draws inspiration from your lifetime of service; your steadfast determination to help those who could not help themselves illustrates what is possible through a genuine love of fellow man.

Having known our family for over 45 years, Peter may well hold the title for "most lunches with Joe." From those conversations, Peter acquired an intimate understanding of my father's life and shares with you glimpses of early days in Vegreville, efforts to make it in Vancouver, service in WWII and expansion of business ventures. And throughout, Peter and his co-authors reveal the little gems of wisdom offered along with lunch.

In a world of incessant chatter, Dad can say so much with so few words. I will not give away anyone's reportage here – you must read the book for yourself – but I feel it is fair game to repeat something that has already been published. In *The Runway of Life*, Peter wrote: "Joe has often said to me that one of life's problems is not that we aim too high and fail. It is that we aim too low and succeed."

Lorne Segal

President, Kingswood Properties Ltd.

CHAPTER 1

LUNCH WITH JOE

"A generous man will himself be blessed
for he shares his food with the poor."
— Proverbs 22:9

My parents Win and Bernie Legge immigrated to Canada with their only son, me, in March 1954 – almost 60 years ago. We settled in New Westminster, B.C. I believe my father was drawn to that particular spot in the Lower Mainland because the name reminded him of Westminster, England. We settled in the Royal City where my father worked for one of the most established firms at that time. The company was called Gilley Brothers Ltd. and their offices were situated on the waterfront facing the mighty Fraser River. The firm sold concrete, bricks and other building supplies that were instrumental in the development of neighbouring communities including both Coquitlam and Port Coquitlam, which were experiencing rapid growth at the time.

I attended Vincent Massey Junior High School (named for Canada's Governor General) and then graduated to Lester Pearson High School, named after Canada's 14th Prime Minister, Lester "Mike" Pearson, who served our country from 1963 to 1968. The two buildings that housed the schools are still in the same location, but the school is now known as New Westminster Secondary School.

My favourite class was English 32, a journalism class. I also worked on and contributed to the school newspaper called *The*

Mike. From that first taste, I was hooked on media; whether it was writing, advertising, administration, sales or layout and production, and for the past 50 years I have been an ardent student of media, primarily in British Columbia.

It most certainly has been an adventure. Nearly 40 years ago, I co-founded Canada Wide Media Limited, which has become the largest, independently owned media company in Western Canada with a staff of 140 talented professionals and a stable of magazines and online properties with a combined readership that numbers in the millions. The company is now 100 per cent family owned with headquarters in Burnaby, B.C.

You could say my entire business life has been in media. First it was *The Columbian* newspaper in New Westminster where I started as a cub reporter and then onto a radio station, CKNW, whose headquarters were on Columbia Street in New Westminster, and then onto sales at radio station CJOR owned by the Chandler family (today the station is part of the Jimmy Pattison radio division in British Columbia).

One of the major accounts assigned to me when I worked at CJOR was the Fields department store chain. The head office of Fields was in store No. 1 at Hastings and Abbott streets right opposite Woodward's on the Downtown Eastside. In a small office in the corner of the store was the boss: Joe Segal. This was in the early 1960s. As Fields was one of my accounts, it was my responsibility to convince Joe to buy an advertising campaign that would air on the station.

CJOR Radio hotliner Pat Burns was the No. 1 talk-show host in the city at the time and the very funny Monty McFarlane was the top morning man. It was a very fast, up-and-coming station and I was proud to be on its sales force.

Sales manager Arnie Nelson had assigned the Fields account to me and his last words of advice were, "Do your homework before you call on Joe Segal, or he will eat you alive." While I was a brash young man of 20, I was a bit intimidated by the prospect of being eaten alive. So, shiny briefcase in hand, I plucked up all of my courage and I went off to sell a radio campaign to Joe Segal.

When I arrived, Joe was sitting in his small office at the back of the store and he made me feel welcome.

"So what have you got for me?" Joe asked after the initial pleasantries had been exchanged.

I went through my "bag of tricks," extolling the merits of radio, touting our vastly improved ratings and highlighting our up-and-coming profile in the city, with the top morning man and a high-profile talk-show host. Joe listened to my entire spiel, paying very close attention to everything I had to say, then as I was finishing, he looked me in the eye and said, "Come back and see me next month and we'll talk."

No sale, but at least he didn't eat me alive.

I went back the next month and repeated my performance, and the month after that, and every month for six months in a row, but still no sale.

Joe even went so far as to tell me, "Peter, you're an excellent salesman, but I'm not buying."

Finally, I spoke up. "You've said that before," I told him. "But I can't be that good. In the past six months you haven't bought anything."

"And I'm not going to," said Joe. "All you've done is to try to sell me what you want me to buy; you haven't once asked me what my needs are."

Wow! What a lesson.

From that moment on, Joe and I hit it off and I have listened closely to all of the advice he has been kind enough to offer. That was almost 50 years ago.

In the 50 years since, I have yet to sell anything to Joe Segal; however, we have partnered on a number of charitable endeavours. After all, Joe is one of the most generous and giving people I know. Both Joe and his wife Rosalie also dine together with my family at some of Vancouver's best restaurants and we have attended many charitable dinners at their beautiful home, all of them for the benefit of worthwhile causes. Some of the special guests at those dinners have included music composer David Foster, musician Kenny G, the Duke of Westminster, the incomparable Yo-Yo Ma and the Archbishop of Canterbury. As a result of the dinners, we've ended up raising millions of dollars for a host of charities in the province and, of course, Joe and Rosalie are always the instigators.

Of course, we have also had many, many lunches over the past few decades in the Four Seasons Hotel, first at Chartwell and now in Yew Restaurant. As most people know, Joe has his own table and when he is in town, he has lunch there virtually every day. If you have the privilege of a lunch with Joe, you show up at 12 noon and Joe comes in around 12:15 p.m. My advice: "Don't be late, because every lunch with Joe is unique, enlightening and an amazing learning experience. You won't want to miss a minute of it."

I always come away from my conversations with Joe with renewed vigour, enthusiasm and a sense of purpose about life. Ask anyone who knows him – Joe just has that effect on you, where you feel rejuvenated, as if you could take on the whole world. I also usually have pages of notes and quotes after a luncheon with Joe, fodder for my many speeches and presentations, sometimes even an entire book, as was the case with *The Runway of Life*, which was inspired by Joe and published in 2005.

No matter the circumstance, Joe is always polite to everyone, uplifting, encouraging and, I might add, one snappy dresser – his collection of suits and ties rivals anything you could find at a first-class clothier like Harry Rosen or Holt Renfrew.

There is no one whose advice I trust more than Joe's. When I was contemplating purchasing the *TV Guide* subscriber base in Greater Vancouver and Victoria (this was a huge deal for Canada Wide Media and I discussed many times with Joe how to go about it), the week we had to make our final decision, I needed his advice. While he didn't know a great deal about the magazine business, I knew that he knew numbers better than almost anyone, so I phoned him in Hawaii. I think he was just finishing breakfast and he said, "Give me the numbers and the projections and then give me a minute." After what seemed like no more than a brief pause, he said, "It's a good deal, write the cheque." And then he hung up.

So, after all these years, what is a two-hour lunch with Joe Segal like?

Joe is humble, caring, kind, full of beans, interested, inquisitive, enquiring; he has a suburban taste in clothes and after the odd glass of wine, it's like being with a kind professor who is a true master of what a meaningful life is all about. But somehow, I never seem to graduate, because I know the lessons and the learning will continue for a long time to come. We talk about the importance of marriage and family, giving back to the community, business, lifestyle, the poor, aging, commitment, regrets, the standard of living, the disenfranchised, our community and most definitely the future.

This book, *Lunch With Joe*, is not a biography; it doesn't cover every aspect of Joe's extraordinary life and career. Instead, it is a collection of stories, experiences and anecdotes I've gathered from more than 20 years of having "Lunch With Joe." This book also includes 90 other authors who have written mini chapters for this book, and I'm grateful to them all.

It's unlikely that theologian John Wesley, born in England on June 28, 1703, had Joe in mind when he wrote the following words, but that doesn't make them any less appropriate to the man whom I am proud to call my friend and mentor:

Earn all you can
Spend all you can
Save all you can
But for heaven's sake
Give all you can

So please, sit back, relax and enjoy *Lunch With Joe.*

CHAPTER 2

VEGREVILLE: THE EARLY YEARS

"If I were starting out again today,
I would look for an opportunity that is going
to teach me something."
— Joe Segal

In the many years that I've known him, Joe hasn't spoken a lot about his parents and the formative years that undoubtedly shaped his character. However, I suspect from the man he turned out to be, that his mom and dad instilled in him some strong values around hard work, responsibility, self-reliance, integrity and, perhaps most particularly, sharing with others.

Joe Segal was born in 1925 in Vegreville, Alberta. When I ask him in the interview we did at the BCBusiness Top 100 luncheon in 2012 if his parents named him Joe in tribute to the two founders of Vegreville, Joseph Benoit Tetreau and Joseph Poulin, he responds, "My mother named me Joe because it was a simple name, easy to remember."

Vegreville, which is located about 64 miles east of Edmonton, is and always has been a small town. The population today is still only about 5,800. It's a farming community, originally settled in 1894 by French-speaking homesteaders who were joined by English- and German-speaking families coming from Eastern Canada. Later came a wave of immigrants from Eastern Europe, many of them from Ukraine, which would account for the giant 31-foot-high Pysanka (Ukrainian Easter egg) erected in the Elks/Kinsmen Park in 1967, which has become an international symbol for the town.

Joe's parents were immigrants too. His father arrived in Canada from Russia in 1896, and in 1908, Joe's parents married in Calgary.

"Canada was different in those days," Joe says. "A bastion of freedom in the world, it represented the dream of all European immigrants. I think most of us here in Canada have some connection to that kind of background. Even if it's a few generations removed, we've heard the stories. My parents, like so many others from different parts of the world, came to Canada with hopes, dreams, the desire to live in freedom and the desire to have an opportunity."

Joe wasn't an only child growing up. He had both an older brother and sister, as well as a younger sister.

"When I was a kid, we were never wealthy," says Joe. "But we were always comfortable. My father loved cars, so we had a Packard with the spare wheels on the running board. It was a beautiful car. My father made a lot of money twice in his lifetime and he lost it twice in his lifetime. The second time he lost it was because he had his money in land. My father had always wanted to buy land, but it wasn't the best timing in the '30s just after World War I. Things got pretty bad for a lot of people at that time."

From the few stories he has shared about his earliest years, I have a feeling that young Joe was a bit of a mischievous chap.

"In those days you didn't have a refrigerator, you had an ice box," Joe tells me. "So everyone would have an ice shed out back of the house with huge ice blocks cut out of the river in the winter and covered in sawdust so you could have ice in the summer. My first great accomplishment was burning down the ice shed when I was four or five years old."

Joe admits that he was not the best student growing up, either. "I was the kind of student who never studied. Never did my homework and never studied but always got through. And that was because I have a retentive memory," he explains.

He also remembers getting strapped in the principal's office at school, though he swears he can't remember why.

"All in all, I had a life that was probably the same as most kids of my generation," says Joe.

"What did you want to be when you grew up?" I ask him during our BCBusiness Top 100 interview, primarily because I always wonder, particularly when it comes to those self-made individuals who achieve great things, if that drive is something they're born with, or something that develops later on.

"All I ever wanted to be is successful," says Joe. "Some guys I grew up with wanted to be a fireman or a police officer or the mayor. I didn't know what I was capable of, so all I wanted to do was be successful, which is why I was always looking out for any opportunities that came my way."

Like most kids, Joe longed for a bicycle of his own when he was growing up.

"I wanted a bicycle, I needed a bicycle, everybody had a bicycle," says Joe. "The bicycle I wanted was $10. I knew I was going to have to save the $10 first. Unfortunately, there weren't many opportunities for a kid like me to make that kind of money.

I was going to have to create my own opportunity. But how on earth was I going to do that?"

Joe did exactly what any entrepreneur worth his salt would do. He looked at the market around him, figured out what was missing and filled the need. How? Well, as it happens, Vegreville is not far from Cold Lake, Alberta, and as Joe tells it, Cold Lake is filled with "large, giant, mammoth whitefish." The fish would be brought into Vegreville frozen and Joe saw an opportunity to make some money selling the fish door to door.

"That was my very first sales job," says Joe. "I peddled those whitefish door to door and I was pretty good at it too because everybody was eating whitefish for a long time and I bought my $10 bicycle. I also learned an important lesson about looking for opportunities that other people aren't interested in."

Things took an unexpected turn for the worse for Joe and his family when Joe was 14 and his father died of a sudden heart attack.

"We go through life and we have certain segments of our life that are forced upon us and it can be difficult to know what to do," says Joe. "Now when you're 14 years old and your father dies, that's something you're certainly not prepared for. I was with him when he passed away. I was working with him painting a house and he suddenly just dropped to the floor and they took him to the hospital where they pronounced him dead . . . and I went home."

Despite the years that have passed, the memories are strong and Joe chokes up while talking about his father.

Eventually, Joe and his family moved to Edmonton.

CHAPTER 3

A FEW IMPORTANT LIFE LESSONS

"If you haven't experienced the bottom,
you won't appreciate the top."
— Joe Segal

When his father died, Joe needed a job.

"We weren't poor, but we weren't wealthy either," he explains. "So if I wanted to do any of the things that my friends were doing, like go out to a movie or get a hamburger, I had to go to my mother and ask her for a dime or a nickel or however much it was. I got tired of that. So I told her, 'I'm going to quit school and get a job,' and that's what I did."

The interview for Joe's very first job took place in a lawyer's office, where he met the owner of a business called the Credit Arcade in Edmonton. The company sold men's suits on a credit plan for a dollar down and a dollar a week. In those days, the only people who bought suits were bankers and undertakers.

As Joe recalls, there were four young men applying for the same job and the lawyer said to them, "Well, I'm going to hire all four of you today, but a year from now there's only going to be one of you left."

"A year later, I was the only one left," says Joe.

I can't say that I was surprised to hear this. One thing I know about Joe, if he's going to commit himself to something, he commits 100 per cent.

That first job selling suits paid $5 a week and Joe worked 60 hours a week, which came out to 8-1/4 cents an hour. Over time, he moved up to $7 per week, followed by $10 per week, then $20. And then the Second World War started and the United States Army Corps of Engineers was commissioned by the U.S. government to build the Alaska Highway as a supply route in case of Japanese attack (they had already bombed Pearl Harbor, proving that an attack on U.S. soil was more than possible). The highway, which would turn out to be America's greatest engineering feat of the modern era, would start in Dawson Creek, B.C., and travel northwest through Whitehorse, Yukon, and then on to Alaska. The entire 1,300-mile road was to be completed in less than a year and Joe heard they were paying big wages to make that happen.

"I applied and wound up as a checker in a gravel pit," explains Joe. "A checker is the guy that's responsible for the success of the gravel pit because the truckers got paid on a yard-mile basis, so if you had 20 yards to truck and you went 50 miles, you got paid according to that, and I was the guy who determined what each truck was carrying and how much they would be paid and I was a kid. I was 17 years old and I was earning $112.50 a week. That was a heck of a lot of money in 1942, I'll tell you."

By the end of his time in Northern British Columbia, Joe had $3,500 saved up and he headed to Calgary for some rest and relaxation.

"I got off the train in Calgary," says Joe. "I had a girlfriend in Calgary, so I got off the train at the Palliser station in Calgary and I had a reservation at the York Hotel, so that's where I was headed. I jumped in a taxi right at the station and along the way the taxi driver asked me where I was coming from, so I told him, 'I've been in the bush, the real bush.' "

"Now you have to remember, I was a 17-year-old kid at this point, so I wasn't very wise to the ways of the world," explains Joe. "So he asks me what there was to do up there in the bush when I wasn't working and I told him, there's nothing to do, so more often than not in the evening there'd be a friendly poker game with the other staff.

"He said, 'Oh, you play poker?'

"And I said, 'Yes.'

"And he said, 'Would you like a poker game?'

"So the taxi driver takes me to the taxi stand and I end up playing poker all night with the taxi driver and one or two other drivers and eventually they've got all of the money that I had saved up," says Joe.

Not knowing what else to do at that point, Joe called his mother in Edmonton and told her he needed to go back to work because he'd lost all of his money. He then asked her to send money to pay for the train.

"She told me flat out, you made the bed, you sleep in it," says Joe. "So there I was, flat-broke in Calgary and my mom wouldn't bail me out . . . so I phoned my sister. She was working at the Army

& Navy in Edmonton at that time and she was making maybe 50 cents an hour. She sent me the money and I never forgot that. That's one of the things you have to remember when you go through life, remember the person who puts their hand out for you. I looked after her for a lot of years later on when she needed someone to be there to take care of her."

But Joe never did use the money to return north in search of a job. After paying off his hotel bill and retrieving his belongings, he didn't have enough money left over to get back to work.

"I had nowhere to go," says Joe. "So it being wartime, I went down and tried to join the Navy, which seemed to me at the time to be the most glamorous of the armed forces because you could actually become a shipwright or something and have a good career out of it."

The problem was, the Navy wasn't just taking guys off the street. The recruiter told Joe he could go ahead and apply and they would get back to him and let him know, probably in about a month or so. But Joe couldn't wait a whole month, so he asked the guy, "What do I do?"

The Navy recruiter suggested that he go down and see the Army recruiter at Mewata Barracks.

"So I went down and I said to the Army recruiter, 'I'd like to join the Army, how long does it take?' and the guy looked at me and he said, 'Buster, you're in!' "

Four months later, after completing basic training in Wainwright, Alberta, and 10 days of bivouac in Debert, Nova

Scotia, Joe found himself in the hold of a ship called the *Mauretania* surrounded by scores of other seasick recruits. The ship, like many other cruise ships of the time that routinely made the transatlantic crossing between London, England, and New York City, had been requisitioned by the British government as a troop ship for the duration of the Second World War. In that time, she travelled 540,000 miles (870,000 km) and carried more than 340,000 troops.

"Did you ever sleep in the hold of a ship in a hammock with no daylight?" quips Joe, referencing his experience of crossing the Atlantic for the very first time. "Neither did I."

Joe landed in Aldershot, England, and spent 10 days there preparing for deployment.

"I was a Private Reinforcement for the Calgary Highlanders and when I arrived, they had just lost half of a platoon in a turnip patch, so that's where they sent me," says Joe. "I was 18 years old. I landed in Belgium and then I travelled from Belgium to Holland, where I spent a winter and often wondered if I would make it so close to the enemy that if you put your hand up they'd shoot it off."

From Holland, Joe crossed the border into Germany and from there he travelled up into the northwestern part of the country.

"When the war ended, I was in some place called Oldenburg, Germany," recalls Joe. "That's where the brigade headquarters was, so that's where we stayed when the war was over, waiting to be sent home. As you can imagine, it took quite a while to get everyone back to Canada following armistice."

When asked what impact his experience in the Second World War had on him as a young man, Joe is quick to answer, "I learned some important life lessons from my experience. First and foremost, that life is such that if you don't treasure it, it can be gone before you know it. A lot of young men lost their lives on that battlefield. We talk about minorities, we talk about the colour of your skin; in those days, in that kind of environment, it didn't matter what the colour of your skin was, the colour of your blood was the same whether you were black, white, Asian, Indian, or what have you. That's why when we go through life we have to understand tolerance."

I also asked Joe if there were times when he was scared.

"I could use a profane word to describe how it felt to be suddenly thrust into the line of fire with no idea what I was doing there. Of course I was scared, you know, advance until you encounter enemy fire, what does that mean? Well, basically, just keep going until they shoot at you. So, are you scared, damn right you are . . . but more than anything else, you're scared of the unknown and I guess that's true of most situations in life. No matter what we're faced with, we can't let fear stop us."

CHAPTER 4

SPARKING THE ENTREPRENEURIAL SPIRIT

"Success is much more a matter of courage than ability."
— Joe Segal

After surviving two-and-a-half years of service overseas during the Second World War, Joe Segal returned to civilian life in Canada. He settled in Vancouver in 1946 with no capital and no trade or profession to fall back on. Even so, he wasn't about to let fate decide what the rest of his life would be like.

"If you remember, when I was 17, my life changed because I lost all of my money in a poker game," says Joe. "Well, when you went overseas, they gave you $5 spending money while you were on the ship. I lost that $5 in a poker game, too."

Most likely, that was the point when Joe finally learned his lesson about poker, because when he returned to Canada with the $1,000 he had earned from his stint in the war, he held onto it. Although as it turned out, he wasn't completely done with gambling.

"When I got out of the Army, I came to Vancouver because my mother was here visiting and the first thing I did was go into the real estate business," explains Joe. "In those days you either had a salesman's license or an agent's license, so I got an agent's license and I was selling coffee shops and corner grocery stores and other small businesses. In those days, the commission was 10 per cent and the average price of the businesses I sold was between

$50,000 and $100,000."

Joe had two partners in the real estate business with him. They were both married guys and they knew a good deal when they saw one, so they would send Joe out to do all of the work, finding potential buyers, showing the properties, making the sale and taking care of the paperwork. Joe was pulling in a lot of money, but there was a problem.

"I would go out and I would get the profits, the commissions, and then I would come back and we would have a crap game at the back of the office and I would lose all my money," says Joe. "They were getting the margin! So I didn't stay in the brokerage business for very long."

Not one to wait for opportunity to knock on his door, Joe decided that the best way to make some money was to look around for something that no one else wanted. Before long, he found what he was looking for. With the war now over, the "something" no one wanted was army surplus.

"I had no money to speak of after leaving the commercial real estate business, maybe $1,000, so I had to be very careful," says Joe. "I always got what no one else wanted, so I had to really think about what I was going to do with it before I bought it because I couldn't afford to make any mistakes."

Joe started out buying odds and ends that he could quickly resell, which allowed him to build up his capital. And then came a big opportunity, a shipment of medical supplies valued at around a million dollars.

"I think I paid $7,000 for it because nobody else knew what to do with it," explains Joe. "When you buy these packages of medical equipment, if you have no idea what a cranium drill is, how do you sell it? I decided the best thing to do would be to put an ad in the paper and address it to hospitals, doctors or anyone in need of medical equipment, announcing that I had new equipment for a third off and used equipment for 50 per cent off. It was good value for those who had a need for it, so I did eventually manage to sell it all."

The positive experience gave Joe confidence in his abilities as a salesman and he quite liked the freedom of being his own man – not relying on someone else for a paycheque. He'd caught the entrepreneurial bug and the good news was that there was no shortage of army surplus for a guy with the inclination to do something with it.

CHAPTER 5

ONE MAN'S SURPLUS IS ANOTHER MAN'S OPPORTUNITY

"If you have love, it's easier."
— Joe Segal

When Joe first met his future wife, Rosalie, it wasn't long after he had returned from serving in the Army and Rosalie was just 16 years old.

"You could say she came off the ship and I took one look at her and knew she was the woman I was going to marry," says Joe. "To back it up a bit though, I came to B.C. after the war because my mother was here and there really was no reason for me to go back to Alberta. So I settled in Vancouver where I had some family, including a cousin who happened to know Rosalie's family. On the day we met, Rosalie had been over on Vancouver Island visiting relatives and she was on her way back home. I just happened to be tagging along with my cousin who was going to pick her up at the ferry. I remember when she walked off the ship, I took one look at her and I said to myself, 'This is the girl of my dreams. I'm going to marry her.' "

Now, if you recall from the previous chapter, this would have been right around the time that Joe had quit his job as a real estate broker and started selling army surplus, so essentially he was a young guy of 22 with no job, no university degree and no resources to fall back on. He did have one thing going for him, however, and that was whatever he may have lacked in terms of resources, Joe made up for in determination as he set out to impress the young Rosalie.

"When I came out of the Army, I had $1,500, which was saved up after two-and-a-half years of service at a rate of about $1.50 per day," explains Joe. "You see, during the war, you didn't need any money. If you wanted a steak, you didn't use money, you traded a pair of boots. So when I received my discharge from the Army, they gave me $1,500 for my service."

What did Joe do with that money? You could say he took a gamble, except this time, finally, he won.

"I bought an automobile just to impress Rosalie," he says. "I had a date and so I spent all my money to impress her. As it turned out, it was a wise investment."

But young Rosalie wasn't the only one Joe needed to win over. Needless to say, Rosalie's parents wanted a young man with a bright future for their daughter and they weren't about to make it easy for Joe to prove that he was worthy.

"I can't say that I blamed Rosalie's mom and dad," says Joe. "They were typical parents. They wanted a doctor or a lawyer or an accountant or perhaps even a politician for their daughter, somebody with a profession and the means to take care of her. So they weren't exactly thrilled with the idea of me wanting to marry their daughter. I mean, there I was still in the Army. I got my army discharge in Vancouver. And so they put obstacles in my way and if I really wasn't honest with my feelings, I would have gone on. But I knew she was the one, so I stayed and they said okay, you wait a year, a year-and-a-half and we'll see. She was still only 16 at the time, so I guess that was a reasonable thing."

With the clock ticking, Joe got busy with more entrepreneurial pursuits. As we talked about in the last chapter, there was no shortage of army surplus available at the time and Joe was quick to spot an opportunity when he saw one, even if he wasn't exactly clear what to do about it.

Faced with the opportunity to purchase 2,000 gallons of olive-green war-surplus paint in five-gallon drums, Joe searched for a need to fill.

"I wound up with this 2,000 gallons of paint and I thought, 'What am I going to do with all of this khaki paint . . . camouflage?' Nobody wants to camouflage their house," he says.

But then Joe came up with a plan.

"I went down and I rented a green Ford panel truck and each morning I would load that truck up with those five-gallon drums and I'd head to somewhere like Ladner and visit the local farmers," says Joe. "I was a pretty good salesman by then and I made my pitch and every barn that hadn't been painted for years ended up painted olive drab. The next day I would do the exact same thing in Chilliwack or somewhere else. The only territory I never went to was Surrey, because I never knew where it was."

By the time Joe ran out of paint to sell, he'd made his mark on the Lower Mainland.

"It was quite the sight to see," laughs Joe. "As you drove along the freeway, all the barns were painted the same olive-green colour."

Joe learned a valuable lesson selling stuff that no one else seemed to want and it was one that would serve him well in his future career as a retailer. Just because nobody else sees the value, doesn't mean something is worthless. Likewise, just because you got something cheap, doesn't mean it has no value; it's what you do with it that really counts. If you're going to sell something, you have to have confidence in yourself and your own abilities.

Asked what made him so good at seeing opportunity where others didn't, Joe responds, "I grew up without a dream. All the other guys in my hometown dreamed of becoming firefighters, policemen or other such heroic figures. My ambition was simply to be successful – wherever that would lead me. I didn't really have a skill or trade to fall back on either, and failure wasn't an option, so I had to be resourceful."

Interestingly, when he first came to Vancouver after the war, his friends from back home told him he was crazy.

"Vancouver's too big," they told him. "You won't make it!"

Joe said, "Heck, it's so big, I can't miss."

And so the beginning of the Joe Segal dynasty in Vancouver began – Joe was always an original, even at the age of 22.

As for Rosalie, Joe must have impressed her parents with his ambition, because a year-and-a-half after their first meeting, the two married.

"And here we are, 64 years later," says Joe.

Together, Joe and Rosalie have four children (Sandra, Gary, Tracy and Lorne), 11 grandchildren and seven great-grandchildren.

CHAPTER 6

OUTSTANDING IN HIS FIELD(S)

"Ultimately, it is persistence that will pay off; forget about perfection."
— Joe Segal

Recognizing he had a talent for buying and selling, Joe continued to build on his success in the surplus business and eventually created a private company under the name of Commercial Distributors and opened an outlet on Main Street in Vancouver where he sold war-surplus supplies. It wasn't long, however, before he was scoping out new horizons to conquer. In 1950, Joe started his first retail store under the Fields name. Although he had originally planned to call the store Thrifty's, at virtually the last minute, he thought better of it.

"Thrifty's would have meant you were dealing with low-end merchandise and I didn't know which way it was going to go with the store, which happened to be located on the corner of Hastings and Abbott in what had been the old Blackburn Market," says Joe. "It wasn't exactly the best location for a fledgling department store, I have to say. There was Woodward's on one side and the Army & Navy store on the other side, but I didn't have so much money at the time and that was a lease that I was lucky enough to get."

Eventually Joe would go on to own the building as well, but in those early years, money was tight and so was the competition, so he had to make smart decisions if he was going to survive in the retail world.

"I decided that I wanted the flexibility to position the store depending on what customers wanted, so I rethought the name, even though it cost me some money up front because I had already ordered all of the advertising under the Thrifty's name," says Joe. "My rationale was, you call it Thrifty and people think price, but you call it Fields and what does it mean? The truth is it could mean anything."

So where did the name Fields come from?

"A lot of people have asked me that over the years," says Joe. "Well, actually I borrowed it. There was a famous retailer in Chicago called Marshall Fields at the time and the company's flagship store was something of a legend, so I decided to take half of it and call my store Fields. That's how I came up with the name. What appealed to me about that was I could have dressed Fields up in a high-end image or down to a thrifty image; there was a lot of flexibility."

Fields started out as a family clothing store and the first location at Hastings and Abbott in Vancouver did well despite being sandwiched between two retail giants, so when the opportunity arose to add a second location on Columbia Street in New Westminster, Joe was eager to expand his empire.

"I bought a company in New Westminster. It was a department store that had been around for a hundred years," says Joe. "Over the years, I bought so many companies just like it where the owners or management wanted to retire, they'd been there so long. This one was Collister's Department Store on Columbia Street and it was a huge store, with two levels and at least 15,000 square feet of retail space – which today would be an insignificant size for a store, but for me at the time, it was huge."

Having bought the store, Joe wasn't sure what his banker would think of the deal or how he was going to finance the operation of his new acquisition, it being almost twice the size of his first Fields store.

"Thankfully, a family member phoned me up and he said, 'You need some help, how about $50,000?'" explains Joe. "'That would be wonderful,' I told him in response to his offer. At that time, $50,000 was a fair amount of money and I can't tell you how much I appreciated that gesture, knowing there was someone who had trust in me. I never had a mentor and I never asked for help, but he offered and we became very close and remained good friends for the rest of his life."

Now with two locations, Joe was able to leverage his buying power and increase the profitability of his operations. The success of the business soon led to a series of stores in the Lower Mainland, including downtown Vancouver, Burnaby and Richmond. The opening of the Capilano Mall location in North Vancouver in 1968 brought the total number of Fields stores to eight.

When asked how he was able to account for the success of a little chain like Fields in a market that included Simpsons-Sears, Woolworths, Kmart and Zellers, Joe replies, "Our marketing policy calls for maximum utilization of sales space rather than frills. We operate primarily on a cash-and-carry basis, thereby limiting the heavy sales and accounting force required with credit buying."

That same year, Joe made the decision to turn Fields into a public company.

"It wasn't until I got to this point that I could really afford any structure," says Joe. "So up to that point, I was the chief cook and bottle washer, I was the buyer, I was the banker, I was the window dresser, I did everything and that's how I learned the integral parts of operating a company."

As CEO of a public company, Joe now had access to the capital he needed to take Fields to a new level and over the next few years, the company grew primarily through acquisition. The first purchase was a small group of family-run stores on Vancouver Island called Spencer's Stores Limited. This was followed by the purchase of the Payless Store in Abbotsford and a department store in Williams Lake called Mackenzie's Limited – all in 1968.

The purchase of stores in small-town communities continued in 1969 with the acquisition of three Hudson's Bay locations in Kimberley, Nelson and Powell River. These locations, together with the Williams Lake store, marked the beginning of a department-store division within Fields that offered a wider range of products than the original clothing stores.

In 1969, Fields expanded its operations even further with the purchase of both manufacturing and import companies. These included a textile mill in Manitoba and a company that imported men's, ladies' and children's clothing from the Far East for wholesale distribution to department stores and independent retailers across Canada.

By 1970, Joe was firing on all cylinders and with net earnings of $1.23 million on sales of more than $21 million – an increase of 40 per cent over the previous year – he continued to make acquisitions in addition to opening an entirely new retail division called Fedco, which operated more like a supermarket (with self-service) than a conventional department store of that era where customers expected to be waited on by sales staff.

"The establishment of Fedco as a department store carrying all lines except furniture and heavy appliances was a natural development in an urban market as an arm or subsidiary of Fields stores, with its traditions as a family-clothing retailer with high sales turnover due to mass buying and its continuing appeal to the public," says Joe.

In 1971, Joe ventured into the specialty market with the introduction of boutique stores that focused on selling pants and tops for young adults who were looking to get in on current fashion trends without spending a lot of money. Five of these stores, called Pants Plus, opened in 1971 along with 15 other new stores, which brought the total number of outlets in the Fields chain to 43. Joe also opened his first store outside of B.C. in the same year, a junior department store in Edmonton.

The year 1972 was equally busy, with the purchase of Marshall-Wells Limited from Gamble Canada for $7.5 million. The large-scale acquisition – Marshall-Wells had 186 franchise outlets in Western Canada as well as a wholesale business – added an entirely new line of business to the company: hardware. The following year, Fields reported that the acquisition had helped push sales to over $68 million, an increase of 89 per cent over the previous year.

With continued acquisitions on the retail side, by 1976 Fields had expanded as far eastward as Saskatchewan and there were 75 stores in the Fields chain (not including the Marshall-Wells outlets). It was quite an empire for a guy who arrived in Vancouver fresh out of the Army with little more than the clothes on his back and a simple desire to be successful.

CHAPTER 7

THE MOUSE THAT SWALLOWED THE ELEPHANT

"Don't risk more
than you can afford to lose."
– Joe Segal

In 1976, right next to Fields store in Brentwood Shopping Centre, there was a Zellers store. Joe's Fields store was 6,000 square feet and the Zellers store was four times the size at 24,000 square feet. That particular Fields outlet was doing a million a year in sales, while the Zellers store was doing just $400,000 in sales.

"Something was definitely wrong with that picture," says Joe during our interview at the BC Business Top 100 luncheon. "I was very surprised to be in the location in the first place," he explains. "Brentwood was the second shopping centre to be built in Vancouver, with Park Royal being the first and I wanted a store in Brentwood, which was being developed by a company called Webber Knapp. This company was a huge real estate developer and they had secured Eaton's as the anchor and although I kept asking, they wouldn't let me in. They didn't want me. Why? First of all, because I wasn't a Triple A covenant and secondly, they didn't think I could provide the right kind of merchandise."

Joe knew that shopping malls were the wave of the future and he was obviously disappointed by the developer's decision, although there wasn't much he could do about it. But then he got a surprise phone call.

"It was about eight months after they'd rejected my offer and they were getting ready to open the shopping centre," says Joe. "Of course, with a high-profile project like that, when you open you want it to be full and vibrant. The problem was, they had an empty retail space and they couldn't find anyone to fill it. So they picked up the phone and they said, 'Well, are you still interested, will you come here?' And I told them, 'I'll do it on one condition: You outfit the store, you get everything ready, including all of the fixtures, you get that store ready on a turnkey basis and I'll bring the merchandise in.'

"We opened Fields in the Brentwood Mall with a Zellers store right next door to us and it didn't take long for me to see that their retail strategy was far from efficient," continues Joe, who thought his competitors should have been doing much better than they were in such a desirable location.

At that time, Zellers was a subsidiary of a U.S. corporation called the W.T. Grant Company, which coincidentally, had just filed for Chapter 11 bankruptcy. As a Canadian subsidiary, Zellers came on the market.

"I've said before that I could never buy anything that anybody else wanted because I could never afford it," says Joe. "Zellers was no exception, even though I expressed an interest early on, I didn't have the kind of money they were looking for, so invariably, the Canadian subsidiary was shopped to every U.S. retailer they could think of, and every significant retailer in Canada as well, including the Hudson's Bay Company and Eaton's. Nobody could see the potential in Zellers, but I could see it. I knew there had to be something."

After the lawyers representing the company ran out of prospects, they came back to Joe.

"I remember, it was Greenshields at that time and they said, 'Do you still want to buy it?' and I said, 'Absolutely!' and they asked, 'How much are you going to pay?' I told them, 'Three dollars a share.' So they said, 'Okay, but you have to get it approved by the bankruptcy court in New York.'"

Joe didn't really understand at the time what he was getting into or how the court process would work; nevertheless he got on a plane with Rosalie and his lawyer and the three of them headed to New York City to buy Zellers.

"The press at the time said, 'That's like the mouse swallowing the elephant'," laughs Joe.

On the way to New York, the plane made a stop in Winnipeg and Joe found himself sitting in the airport waiting room next to a couple of guys talking about something that sounded very familiar to him.

"One of them was a lawyer and the other was the president of a relatively big Canadian retailer [which also happened to be a subsidiary of a large U.S. company] and they're talking about Zellers and how they're on their way to New York to buy Zellers," says Joe. "So now I knew that I had competition and not just that, but competition with deep pockets; this was a multi-billion-dollar company."

Joe and the competition arrived in New York and met at court the next morning, where the judge laid out the facts. "Well, we have two parties interested in the company," the judge said. "So it's a bidding contest and the high bid is going to win it."

The problem for Joe was that he knew he had a limit as to how much he could afford to pay for Zellers. He also knew that the competition faced no such problem.

"I was fortunate that the Bank of Montreal had confidence in me and they gave me a line of credit of $50 million," says Joe. "When the bidding started, the judge asked me how much I was going to pay and I said $30 million. The competition countered with $32 million. I said $33 million and then they said $34 million and I thought, 'I'm going to run out of money before I know it.' So we got to $38 million and then I said to the judge, 'Your honour, my bid is unconditional and you will have a cheque when you accept it. Is their bid unconditional?' "

The judge turned to the competition and posed the question.

Now you know that Joe is one smart guy, so you've probably already guessed that he had a strategy to turn his disadvantage into an advantage – and he was pretty sure he knew what would happen next.

"We know if you accept our bid, it will get approved," his competitor told the judge. "However, it requires board approval and the chairman is fishing at the present time, so we won't be able to get that for a week or two."

Joe knew it was time to give a little push.

"Your honour," he said. "My bid is legitimate and it's immediate and unconditional."

"Will you please let us adjourn for a week?" the judge asked Joe.

"No," said Joe, knowing full well he would lose the deal if he didn't keep the pressure on.

"Will you at least let us adjourn until tomorrow?" asked the judge.

"Okay," said Joe.

"We'll reconvene tomorrow at 10 a.m.," said the judge.

Back at the hotel, Joe received a surprise phone call from the lawyer representing his competition.

"We'd like to have breakfast tomorrow," the lawyer told Joe.

"What time?" asked Joe.

"Six o'clock," responded the lawyer.

"What are we going to talk about?" asked Joe.

"You have breakfast with us and you'll find out," said the lawyer.

Knowing this wasn't just any lawyer, but one representing a major Canadian law firm, Joe was both perplexed and a little curious about what they wanted to discuss.

"Okay, we'll have breakfast," said Joe.

Normally, Joe isn't the kind of guy to get up for breakfast at six in the morning – he's more of a lunch guy as you may have surmised from the stories contained in this book – but he woke up early and went to the breakfast meeting where the lawyer got straight to the point.

"Look, you're not going to get this company," he told Joe. "You don't have enough money. We're going to buy this company and all you're doing is costing us money. So, we'll give you $4 million and you can pack your tent and go home."

Four million dollars was a lot of money in 1976 and Joe was taken aback, but he wasn't about to let anyone push him around.

Joe looked the lawyer straight in the eye and said, "I think you're circumventing the law. I'll see you in court."

Both parties returned to court at 10 a.m.

"Is your bid unconditional?" the judge asked the competition.

"No, we can't make an unconditional offer," they replied.

So the judge turned to Joe and said, "Okay, you've got the company and I hope I never see you in this courtroom again."

On July 27, 1976, Fields acquired a controlling interest in Zellers and Joe became chairman of the board of Zellers. During the next three years, under Joe's leadership, Zellers sales doubled without opening a single new location and revenues went from $350 million to $800 million. During that same time, through a reverse takeover, Fields Stores became a subsidiary of Zellers.

Having successfully swallowed the elephant and proven that he could turn a business around in short order, Joe set his sights on even bigger game. This time it was the Hudson's Bay Company, also known as HBC.

"I recognized the Hudson's Bay Company as a sleeping giant with a tremendous, understated balance sheet," explains Joe. "Its breakup value was huge, except that I had no intention of breaking it up. In merging it with Zellers, my vision was to create the largest retailing entity in Canada, covering all ends of the market."

In 1978, Joe approached HBC's president and proposed that Zellers buy a 51 per cent stake in the company. The offer came as a total surprise to the company. Not entirely sure that Joe was serious, HBC's president countered that any serious bid would have to be for cash and 100 per cent control of the company. Much to HBC's surprise once again, within days, Joe had put together an offer on precisely those terms.

Recognizing what Joe had accomplished with Zellers and taking into account the fact that the two companies operated in different areas of the retail market, HBC decided the most sensible option was for it to buy Zellers instead. When the deal was finalized in 1979, HBC gained a controlling interest in Zellers, and Joe, having become a major shareholder in the company, joined the board of the Hudson's Bay Company, the world's oldest retailer.

"In the end, I didn't particularly care which of the two companies emerged on top," said Joe. "As long as it was done."

CHAPTER 8

JOE'S STRATEGY FOR SUCCESS

"Put more in than you take out,
and it will never run dry."
— Joe Segal

Fifty years ago, Joe shared his definition of success in a speech.

"For me, success is a sense of wellbeing, a sense of belonging, a sense of contributing and having a good relationship with your peers. At the same time, financial success gives you the ability to maintain the standard of living you want."

Here's a breakdown of Joe's strategy for success (which is as valid today as it was 50 years ago):

1. Before anything else, an entrepreneur has to recognize market opportunities. "There is plenty of opportunity in this city – all you have to do is say, 'Hey, what's missing in the marketplace?' And once you recognize what's missing you say to yourself, 'I can fill that need.' "

That's exactly what Joe has always done, whether it was selling fish door to door or taking over the Zellers department stores, Joe always saw potential where others saw problems.

2. Once the opportunity has been seized, flexibility is the operative word. "If you're going to develop a master plan and follow that master plan without altering it as you go along, you're never going to make it because the world is constantly changing around you, which means circumstances change and

so the plan has to change also."

Joe is nothing if not flexible in his execution.

Most people are dogmatic and say things like, 'This is the way we've always done it in the past,' or 'That's just the way it is.' Not Joe, who built an empire by doing things that others thought impossible. "Most people simply aren't imaginative enough," says Joe. "Human nature always wants to be right and very often people will stick with the safe road when they should be carving their own path and saying, 'We can find a better way.' "

3. The next step is to preserve capital. Joe always says, "Leave something in the pot to grow."

You have to have money to make money and Joe is an expert when it comes to leveraging his resources. "If I can digest the risk, I'm entitled to the reward," Joe explains. "But if I risk everything and I lose, it's my own fault because I've put myself out of the game. If you want chicken soup, you've got to make sure you've got a chicken in the pot."

4. All the capital in the world won't ensure success if you can't attract the right kind of people to run the shop. According to Joe, "Good staff are the strength and fibre of the business."

Joe has always been smart about surrounding himself with competent men and women to take care of the day-to-day running of his operations, which allows him to do what he does best, make deals.

5. Keep looking forward. "Not everything I did was highly successful," explains Joe. "But most things were, so remember to

always look to the future."

Everyone makes mistakes; it's part of being human and the best way to learn. Most entrepreneurs won't make the same mistake twice and they are always looking forward to the next opportunity.

6. "Lastly, success means being prepared to make sacrifices – but not so much so that you lose yourself."

Joe's advice: Find the right balance for you. Don't deprive yourself of personal time or pleasure. Stay close to your family and your kids – that is ultimately what is most important. Obviously, making a living and being a success is important, but don't risk family to succeed. No matter how rich or how poor you may be, if you have the love of your family, you have succeeded.

CHAPTER 9

A CAPITAL IDEA: THE BIRTH OF KINGSWOOD CAPITAL

"Too many times in life,
we see a need but hesitate to act on it."
— Joe Segal

In 1979, Joe Segal formed Kingswood Capital Corporation to expand his operations into new areas, including venture capital financing, real estate development, manufacturing and the acquisition of companies that he could turn around. Kingswood's first purchase was a men's clothing manufacturer that ultimately became Mr. Jax (Ladies) Fashions. During the early years of Kingswood, the company acquired many other clothing manufacturing companies as well.

In 1985, Joe expanded into a whole new sector that he hadn't really anticipated when he acquired national retailer Collegiate Sporting Goods from Imasco.

"I got a phone call one day from a company called Imasco, which was owned by Imperial tobacco," explains Joe. "They had a chain of sporting goods stores called Collegiate Sporting Goods and they didn't know what to do with them."

Collegiate had been losing $4 million to $5 million a year and they asked Joe, "Will you take it over? You've sold Zellers and you're pretty much retired."

"And I said, 'Do I need another problem?'" recalls Joe. "But they said, 'Come and look at it anyway.'"

Joe flew to Toronto and when he arrived, the company had

taken a room at the Bristol Hotel at the airport and there were 27 executives in that room and they wanted to sell him the company.

"The company was losing about $5 million per year and they were perpetuating the problem instead of addressing the problem," says Joe. "The end result was, it was a logical business in the right place, so I said, 'I'll take the company provided you carry the paper. That way, if I fail, you fail and if we win, we win together.' "

Joe bought the company and within one year, he took it from a $5-million-a-year loss (which had been going on for several years) to a $1-million profit. How?

"It was common sense," says Joe. "What's the point in retaining inventory on your books if it has no value? So we cleaned house and instead of having $50 million or $60 million of unsalable inventory, we had $10 million of desirable inventory. Despite what some people might think, retail isn't that complicated. To be a successful retailer, you need the right merchandise, in the right place, at the right time, at the right price . . . and then you'll be successful."

That's the same kind of common sense Joe has applied to every business he's ever run and it's exactly what has made him so successful.

"As I've explained before, I could never really afford to buy what everyone else wanted, so I've made a habit of buying what no one else wanted," concludes Joe. "And the funny thing is sometimes, like in the case of Collegiate, they actually beg you to take it off their hands when it's a perfectly good business. You just need to know how to run it."

While telling the story during the BC Business Top 100 luncheon, Joe joked with the audience that it certainly wasn't his sporting goods expertise that helped him turn the company around: "I was never on a pair of skis in my life, I was never on a tennis court. The only thing I ever did recreationally probably was to count money."

In 1986, Joe merged Collegiate with Sports Experts, becoming chairman of both companies, and in 1988, he played an instrumental role in the $150-million acquisition of Block Bros., a Western Canadian company in the land development and property investment field, which now operates as First National Properties.

Over the years, Joe has rescued and reinvigorated a large number of retail businesses. Likewise, he has bought and sold a lot of commercial real estate. His first foray into real estate came when he had a surplus $100,000 from his retail business that he used to buy a building.

"That was at the time that the *Vancouver Sun* and the *Vancouver Province* had merged," says Joe. "They had built a new building, if you remember, on Granville and 7th, so the building at the corner of Cambie and Hastings became available for sale. It seemed like a nice building, but I had never owned a building that size. I made an offer on it, $100,000, and they countered back. Then the building behind that one, located on Cambie and Pender, also came on the market and I wanted that, too. So I ended up with two great buildings opposite Victory Square."

In typical fashion, Joe bought both buildings because no one else wanted them given their proximity to the problems of the Downtown Eastside.

"Anyway, I bought the buildings because nobody else liked the area, but then I wasn't sure what to do with them," continues Joe. "As I mentioned, the first one was this former newspaper building and they didn't even broom-sweep it. That's something that goes into a contract, but I didn't know that at the time. There was newsprint everywhere and dirt, a lot of dirt. The former owner said to me, 'Well, you own it now. It's yours.' So I said, 'Okay.' "

Joe went through the building floor by floor.

"They used to print the comics, colour comics and these printing presses were up on big bunkers made out of concrete," says Joe. "I was curious as to what was under these big printing presses and under the bunkers, so I went in and I took a look and I saw what looked like a huge painting or portrait or something wrapped in this very fragile newsprint. I took it out and I opened it."

Inside the paper was what turned out to be a very valuable original painting of the founder of Southam Press.

"But I didn't like the painting and I wasn't sure what to do with it. After all, he was no relative of mine," says Joe. "I decided that maybe he had a relative or someone else that would want the painting, so I went through the phone book to find somebody by the name of Southam. I found a Southam entry and I picked up the phone."

Joe called the number and the phone was answered by Gordon Southam.

"Are you related to this guy?" Joe asked, reading out the name that was printed on the frame of the painting.

"'Yes, he's my grandfather," Gordon told him.

"I've got this painting here and it's a Southam painting. Would you like it?" asked Joe.

"Well, yes, what's it going to cost me?" replied Gordon.

"The price of a cab fare," said Joe. "Come on down and pick it up."

Based on that first interaction and Joe's act of kindness, he and Gordon became very good friends and remained so for many, many years until 1998 when Gordon Southam died.

More often than not over the years, Joe's instincts for recognizing value have served him well. He's developed a multimillion-dollar real estate portfolio that includes a number of iconic buildings such as the Grosvenor Building or the Kingswood Shaughnessy, which was designed and built by his son Lorne Segal.

But no matter how attractive a deal might be, Joe looks at each project and measures the risk/reward ratio.

"If I can digest the risk, I'll take a shot and I'm entitled to the reward," he explains. "But you have to be able to make a decision. If you can make a decision and make it quickly, you're at an advantage. If you dilly-dally or your banker won't listen to you, you'll miss out."

Despite his talent for deal making, Joe is as likely to donate a building as sell it.

In 2002, he and his family donated the former Bank of Montreal heritage building located on Granville Street in downtown

Vancouver to become the home for Simon Fraser University's graduate management programs. In recognition of the donation, the school was renamed the Segal Graduate School of Business.

Likewise, in 2006 the Olympic Organizing Committee went looking for new offices for their rapidly expanding job of planning the 2010 Vancouver Winter Olympics and discovered there was only one site in the entire city capable of meeting their needs – a building located at 3585 Graveley Street and owned by Kingswood Capital. Instead of taking advantage of the opportunity to make a profit on the deal (there were at least nine firm offers for long-term leases for the building at the time), Joe and his family sold the building to the City of Vancouver for $11 million less than the appraised value, on the condition that VANOC would receive a generous deal for the duration of their lease. Joe said it was his family's way of contributing to the success of the Olympics.

Joe is always philosophical when he talks of his many real estate and investment wins and he's the first to admit that there have been a few losses as well. He's philosophical about those too.

"You don't look back," he says. "You live in the present, you look to the future, and you remember the past, but don't try to recreate the past. It's gone. What you can't change, you don't try to change."

In May 2007, Joe was inducted into both the Canadian Business Hall of Fame and the B.C. Business Hall of Fame. Today, he is still highly involved with and works full time at Kingswood Capital, as well as actively sitting on multiple boards of both charitable institutions and businesses.

As for Kingswood Capital, it is currently involved in extensive real estate developments in British Columbia, Alberta and Washington State and the family-owned business controls diversified manufacturing companies such as Arpac (steel racking and lift-truck distribution), EZ Rect Manufacturing (steel shelving and gas-fired boilers), and Storkcraft Manufacturing (juvenile furniture). Joe is also a financial investor in Channel M multicultural television station in Vancouver. In 2005, Joe converted his Sterling Shoes Corporation (originally purchased from a receiver) into an income trust. Sterling Shoes operated 120 retail stores under various trade names until the company was sold to Town Shoes in 2012.

CHAPTER 10

THE RUNWAY OF LIFE: THE GOSPEL ACCORDING TO JOE

"The common traits among all successful people are desire, determination and confidence."
– Joe Segal

It was during a lunch with Joe a number of years ago now, that he first shared his idea about the Runway of Life, which is based on the fundamental truth that no matter how you look at it, we all have a limited amount of time to accomplish all the things we want to do in this life. Those lunches, which over the years had become a habit that I think both Joe and I enjoyed, usually took place at Chartwell Restaurant (and later at Yew Restaurant) in the Four Seasons Hotel in downtown Vancouver, where Joe is such a fixture that he has his own table.

During many of the lunches, when there wasn't a particular issue at hand, I enjoyed sitting back and listening to Joe talk about his life and the lessons that experience has taught him and it was on one such occasion, while Joe was expanding on his philosophy of life, that I got the idea for my book, *The Runway of Life*.

"Many people think of life as a road or a highway," Joe said to me that day. "And that may be true insomuch as there are many unexpected twists and turns and sometimes you get lost or end up at a destination that wasn't on the map. But if you think about it, a highway can go on forever, and life just isn't like that. Life is more like a runway – because at some point you're going to run out of asphalt."

At this point, Joe picked up a napkin off the table and drew a horizontal line across it. At the beginning of the line he put a zero and at the end of the line he put the number 90.

"This is the Runway of Life," Joe told me. "And that number at the end is how old I expect to be when I meet my maker." Next, Joe wrote his current age on the line and turned to me. "The part of the line between zero and your current age, that's history, it's done, so forget about it."

Then he pointed to the section of the line between his current age and where he expects his runway to end. "The distance between where I am now and the end of my runway, that's all I've got to work with. So I have to ask myself, 'What am I going to do with the time that I have?' and whatever my answer is to that question, that's what I need to stay focused on."

I looked down at the napkin in Joe's hand and saw how short the section of the line was, then I thought about my own runway and started to break it down. If I'm fortunate enough to live to 90 years, that would mean just 25 more birthdays, 25 Christmas dinners with my family and 25 more glorious summers.

"Now most people trick themselves into thinking they have more time than they actually do," Joe continued. "It used to be we could expect to live three score and ten, that's 70 years. Now we have great medicine, so people start to think, 'I'm halfway there when I get to 50,' but that's not true. The average lifespan today, I'd call it 80, when you have the ability to really live – lots of people exist beyond 80, but they don't have the capacity to live their life the way they would want to. Now you realize, 50 is not halfway, it's actually 5/8ths of the way and you know how much that is? It's 62.5 per cent. Suddenly, what you do with that runway becomes very important and the lighter your load, the easier it will be to see and do all that you want to. So you live for today and don't worry about the past because life is really a lot shorter than we think."

I realized in that moment that Joe was right, no matter what we have accomplished in the past – or how successful we have been – what really matters is the time we have ahead of us and what we choose to do with what is left of our runway of life. In that one simple yet powerful illustration, Joe had summed it up, and I told him right then, "This is a compelling idea and it would make a great book."

The Runway of Life was published in 2005 and since that time, the theme has become one of the key messages in my speaking engagements where I start out by drawing the runway on a piece of paper or a white board and filling in some numbers. Then, I remind my audience that all of our runways come to an end – sometimes with little or no warning.

The question for all of us is, "How much time are we willing to waste?" Minutes? They quickly turn into hours and those hours have a tendency to become days before we know it and suddenly the days turn into weeks and all too soon, the years slip by and we wonder where all the time went.

When I was preparing to write *The Runway of Life*, I read some comments written by a young entrepreneur in Toronto. He was talking about how our success in life is determined more by what we choose to focus our energy on each day than it is by being the first, the best or the brightest. He offered Terry Fox as an example, saying, "A one-legged kid with cancer runs halfway across Canada while millions complain that there's nothing on TV tonight."

Joe is not one to waste time. Pretty early in life Joe made the decision to use only what works for him, to build an extraordinary life and to set an example that others could follow.

I've heard it said that great companies are not built by individuals who rely on somebody else to take care of them. They are built by men and women who rely on themselves, who dare to shape their own lives, who have enough courage to blaze new trails; individuals with enough confidence in themselves to take the necessary risks. As I recounted earlier in this book, when Joe left Alberta as a young man to come to Vancouver, friends said, "It's so big you can't succeed." Joe said, "It's so big I can't miss."

The world is in need of leaders. Countries need leaders. Businesses need leaders. Communities need leaders and families need leaders. Joe has often said to me that one of life's problems is not that we aim too high and fail. It is that we aim too low and succeed. No one could ever accuse Joe of aiming too low; he is an inspiration to me and everyone else who has had the good fortune to benefit from his generosity of spirit and his wisdom. In every field of endeavour, be it the building of his business empire, his contributions to more good causes than I can name, his championship of Simon Fraser University or the wise counsel he has shared with generations of entrepreneurs in this city, Joe's stamp of leadership is everywhere.

"If I can do it, anyone can do it," he often tells me.

That's leadership; that's Joe.

As I mentioned at the beginning of this chapter, the lunch where Joe introduced me to the Runway of Life took place a number of years ago. When I interview Joe in 2012 during the BCBusiness Top 100 luncheon, I ask him what it's like to be approaching that number he had originally written on the napkin.

"I'm happy with my runway and the choices I've made," Joe tells me. "If you said to me today, 'If you had it to do all over, Joe, what would you change?' The answer would be 'nothing.' "

I also ask him what his goals, dreams and ambitions are for the next five, 10 or even 15 years.

"What is my ambition?" says Joe. "To live! To live! I want to be here, what else is there for me? You can do anything you want to do if you really want to do it. I intend to be here for the next five or 10 years and keep my driver's license."

CHAPTER 11

MENTORSHIP

"Alone, you are only as good as your reach –
you must join hands with others."
– Joe Segal

As one of the most successful entrepreneurs in Canadian history, Joe has a lot of wisdom to share and he is always generous with his time. From his table at the Four Seasons, Joe has dispensed his much sought-after advice to all comers for more than 30 years. If you made a list of all those people, as likely as not, it would read like a veritable who's who of successful people in Vancouver, many of whom have generously shared their stories for this book – thank you all!

Joe doesn't pick and choose whom he gives advice to because he will be the first to tell you, the advice is free and that's not what's going to make someone a success. It's up to each and every person what they choose to do with Joe's advice, and that is what makes it golden.

"Success is much more a matter of courage than ability," he always says. "I can't abide negligence. If someone is capable of a higher level of achievement and they are only doing what they have to do to get by, then that's their choice. To each their own, I guess."

Joe isn't just throwing out a cliché when he says this; however, he's also referencing the title of one of his favourite songs. As a young man, when he was courting the beautiful Rosalie, they used to go out to a supper club and they would dance to the song, "To

Each His Own" by the Ink Spots.

Rosalie's father didn't understand what his daughter saw in Joe. "He'll never amount to much," he once told her.

Joe was determined to prove him wrong.

"If you want the good life, you need to be able to afford it," Joe says of his determination to be a success. "I definitely wanted the good life and I wanted to marry Rosalie, so failure wasn't an option for me. Besides, to my mind, failure is simply a lack of resourcefulness; you only fail when you give up. Failure happens when there's a lack of creativity, passion, determination or commitment. I had all of those things in spades, so there was no way I was going to fail."

And he didn't.

"After all, who doesn't want to live the good life?" Joe always says with a smile and a wave of his hand.

As someone who motivates others as a public speaker, one of my favourite things over the years when having lunch with Joe has been to get his perspective on what makes a person successful. So when I ask him one day what one characteristic is a surefire indicator that someone will turn out to be a successful person, he was quick to answer.

"Tenacity!" he exclaims. "The ability to pick yourself up, regroup and keep going when you encounter obstacles on your Runway."

According to Joe, making mistakes is a fact of life and also a great learning opportunity.

"The secret to success, the thing that many people never figure out," Joe tells me time and again, "is that we all miss the mark many times before we find success. I've always believed that experience is the best teacher. I say, show me a person who is a failure and I will show you someone who gave up while success still lay before them. Then show me a person who is a success and I will show you someone with many mistakes behind him."

Joe concludes that while having a special talent or ability is no doubt a great advantage, unless it is developed and applied, it is no guarantee of success. Likewise, acquiring specialized knowledge or training can also contribute to your success; however, it is only valuable to the extent that you are prepared to apply it.

If you remember back to the first chapter of this book, I told you the story about how I first met Joe when I was selling advertising for the radio station CJOR and he had his office in the back of one of his Fields department stores. Now you may have wondered when you read that story why I kept going back to see Joe again and again despite the fact that he kept telling me he wasn't going to buy any advertising from me. The truth is I admired the man – he started out in business with very little money, but a whole lot of determination and ambition – and I wanted to be like him. I wanted to be successful and I figured the best way to learn how to do that was by modelling myself after someone like Joe, who was living the kind of life I wanted for myself.

I think the other reason I returned was because Joe always encouraged me. He told me to dream big and then go after my dream with everything I had in me. Although he never bought any advertising from me, Joe told me that he admired my persistence. He seemed to think that that persistence could more than make up for whatever I lacked in experience or financial resources. In the 50 or more years since, I've always kept that lesson in mind when I was faced with a difficult task.

In the end, some of the most successful people in the world, including Joe himself – those who have excelled beyond what most of us could even imagine – are not the most talented or even the most educated. They are the individuals who are able to stand committed to one goal or purpose, come hell or high water.

Being a self-made man, over the years Joe's wisdom has been much sought after for all sorts of matters. Particularly those related to business. If there were a poster-boy for "paying it forward," that would be Joe, who is constantly approached by those looking to follow in his footsteps. Several years ago, one such young man sent Joe a note requesting an opportunity to meet with him and ask for advice – enclosed with the note was a $50 bill.

Being the guy that he is, I know Joe would have met with the young man without the $50 and of course, upon meeting him for lunch, Joe returned the money and asked how he might be of service. During their lunch, the young man posed his question to Joe: "How can I become wealthy without borrowing a lot of capital?"

"You can either go into real estate or the stock market," was Joe's advice. "You don't need capital for either of those careers. What you do need is a willingness to work hard, the ability to put in long hours and the discipline to learn the business."

The lunch ended and both men went their separate ways.

Some years later, the young man showed up at the Segal Graduate School of Business at Simon Fraser University just as the university was renovating the building, which as I mention elsewhere in this book, had once been a bank and was generously donated by the Segal family to house the university's management programs. Having heard that the young man (now somewhat older) was visiting, Joe decided to give him a personal tour of the facility from top to bottom and at the same time find out how the young man had fared in the intervening years.

As they walked from floor to floor and room to room, Joe learned that the advice he had given the young man had paid off. He had gone into the stock market and was now a big success. Hearing that there were still a couple of classrooms that needed sponsorship money to complete the renovations, the young man decided on the spot that he would give $200,000 to sponsor one of the rooms on the second floor as his way of saying thank-you to Joe for taking the time to listen and offer some thoughtful advice years earlier.

Such is the life and generosity of Joe, who has provided the same wise counsel and inspiration to generations of aspiring young men and women in our community.

I can think of no one whose example as a role model more clearly embodies the Jewish sage Hillel's words than Joe:

If I am not for myself, who will be for me?

If I am only for myself, who am I?

If not now, when?

As we wound up our BCBusiness Top 100 luncheon interview in 2012, I hit Joe with one last barrage of questions, which he gracefully answered:

What advice would you give us to give our children?

"Keep an open mind," he says. "Don't get hung up with a focus that becomes all consuming. I would rather be 25 starting out without a dime than be where I am today with more money than I can ever use. But you can't do that, can you? If you're young, make a few mistakes, but try. Don't get slotted. You know, I've said a hundred times, in your 20s you can make a lot of mistakes, in your 30s you can still make a few, in your 40s maybe one, in your 50s, it's treacherous."

What's the most important thing for a young person just starting out today?

"The one thing you have to do as you go through life is learn," advises Joe. "Learning is not necessarily out of a textbook. Learning is experience. Like a child who puts their hand on a hotplate, they don't do it twice. So as you go through life, you gain from experience. I can read a lease as well as lawyer, but I'm not a lawyer. I can read a financial statement as well as an accountant, but I'm not an accountant. It comes from experience, but you have to pay attention; otherwise it goes in one ear and comes out the other."

What qualities do you look for in senior executives in your companies?

"At one time, I employed as many as 15,000 people and there was always someone that had more capability than me and that's what I look for," says Joe. "If I were to hire an executive today, I would want someone who is better than me rather than someone that I can suppress. When you run a business there is a tendency to suppress talent to make yourself look good. That's a big mistake. I've seen lots of people who try to hold down the people around them thinking that it makes them look better. It doesn't. You can never make yourself look good at the expense of somebody else. What's more, why would you hire someone if you weren't going to make use of their talents and abilities?"

Who has inspired you?

"That's a hard question to answer because you know I've really been a loner most of my life because I've had to be," muses Joe. "You know, I grew up in the small town of Vegreville and I didn't have too many friends and even later on after I came out of the Army, I kind of followed my own path. So my confidants when I was growing my business were probably my bankers. If I was going to do a deal and I had to borrow some money, I would go to my banker and say, 'What do you think?' And if he didn't like it, never mind that he wouldn't give me the money, I didn't want the deal because there was something wrong with it. He was smarter than me. So I can't think of any one individual."

Finally, I ask Joe if he has any regrets in life.

"You don't look back," he tells me. "You live in the present, you look to the future, and you remember the past, but don't try to recreate the past. It's gone. What you can't change, you don't try to change." That philosophy is part of a larger life lesson that Joe is happy to share with anyone who hopes to follow in his footsteps as an entrepreneur. "Life is a runway," he likes to say. "It starts when you are born. It ends when you die. What you do along that runway is up to you."

CHAPTER 12

JOE'S PEARLS OF WISDOM

"My ambition was to be successful, wherever that would lead me."

— Joe Segal

Joseph Segal is a self-made man who believes that experience is a great teacher. "I had a lot of advantages because I never had a business degree," Joe has always said. "So I had no preconceived notions about what should be or shouldn't be, about what's right and what's wrong."

Over the years Joe has mentored hundreds of budding entrepreneurs, including Lululemon CEO Chip Wilson, sharing with them his many "pearls of wisdom." Here then, are 25 of his best gems:

1. Expecting someone else to solve your problems is unrealistic and you don't learn a damn thing from it. When you figure out what the question is, then you will be ready to find the answer.

2. Believe it or not, the best opportunities don't come in a package with a bow. More often they present themselves in the form of a problem. Successful people are those who are willing to put their neck on the line and take a risk – they see a need and act decisively to find a way to fulfill it.

3. If you believe you'll win, you're already halfway there. The most common thing that holds us back is our own negative thoughts or expectations.

4. Desire provides the motivation to get you started,

determination keeps you going when you encounter obstacles, and confidence gives you the courage to see it through to the end, even when others don't believe in you.

5. For the most part, there simply isn't enough time in the world for us to worry about perfection. Besides, perfection isn't about doing a good job; it is about being in control and an overbearing need to be right. It is a far better thing to be persistent, find a goal that captures your imagination and strive to achieve it.

6. Free will is a beautiful thing, yet it comes with responsibility and accountability. The sum of your life rests on your shoulders. Only you can decide your fate through the priorities you set, the decisions you make, the efforts you spend, the sacrifices you make. What you choose for today will determine all of your tomorrows. Act accordingly!

7. Competing in business in today's globalized world is a battle of wits; more than ability, it requires courage. But don't be mistaken, courage is not the lack of fear, it is fear plus action. Courage comes from deep within the heart and flushes away the paralysis created by fear; it is the willingness to reach beyond one's comfort zone. Courage comes in many forms, not only from thoughts and deeds of greatness, but in the everyday art of being true to your word. It is a skill that can be learned and strengthened through practice and it begins with the question, "What would I be doing if I were 10 times bolder?"

8. Great leaders are those who, when faced with a challenge, can look within themselves, assessing both their strengths and

their weaknesses and then take action or make strategic decisions in accordance with what they see.

9. It's not easy to keep priorities in perspective; however, the ability to do so will be a great factor in determining how quickly you achieve your goals. Just as we must choose one specific career from the many, we must also be discerning about which situations we need to deal with personally, which we should delegate and which we should ignore altogether. Being able to filter out that which is not relevant frees us up to give more attention to what is important.

10. Ever wonder why some of the most successful people in business — the ones who manage to stay on top for decades — are those who have, at one time or another, failed magnificently? I believe it is because experience is the best teacher and if you are really going to succeed at anything, you have to know — when your big plan blows up in your face — how to pick yourself up and start building again.

11. If you choose to focus on giving rather than taking — creating a sense that you have more than you need — you will always have an atmosphere of abundance in your life. What's more, if you don't need something, why not give it away to someone who does?

12. Remember how as a child, whenever you went out, your parents told you to stick together and hold hands to cross the street? Well, nothing has changed. Joining up with others — sharing both risks and resources — gives us courage and allows us to play to our strengths, accomplishing far more than we could ever do alone.

13. Hierarchies work great in the military, not so great in business. Having too many levels of management often means the person at the top – the one making the decisions – has no idea what the people in the trenches are thinking and doing. If you're in charge, make a point to keep communication flowing in both directions and get the word out that you have an open-door policy.

14. Far too many people complicate their lives by worrying about little things and never choosing a direction or purpose. My philosophy is very straightforward: the simplest way is the best way. Stick to the basics, stay focused on your goals, treat others with respect, speak the truth, be thankful for what you have and don't be afraid to help out others when you can.

15. When times get rough, those who make the mistake of withdrawing and trying to hide the problem often simply make the situation worse and end up very depressed. The sooner you come to terms with your problem, the sooner you will be able to get back on top.

16. All in all, love is a rare commodity in this world. It doesn't come often. When it does we should be prepared to recognize it. If you are fortunate enough to find someone to love, consider what a privilege it is that this person has found you worthy of sharing their universe.

17. The world is constantly changing. You must learn and grow continually to keep up. The most successful people avail themselves of every opportunity to learn. It matters not whether you were born rich or poor, knowledge is the great equalizer.

No matter what you come from, if you pursue knowledge, it will change your fate.

18. You may think of age 65 and retirement as the ultimate goal in your life, but when it has come and gone, then what? Believe me, some of the best years of life come after 65, and yet, so many people do not plan for what they hope to accomplish during this time.

19. If you think you have no right to be successful, you are right! Lack of confidence is often a form of shame; it can be very debilitating to one's progress in life. Confidence is an acknowledgement of your self-worth. If you do not value yourself, others will follow your example and they will not value you either.

20. If you just seek money, you'll fail. If you seek success, you'll get the money . . . and the sense of fulfillment that comes with challenging yourself and achieving your goals.

21. Money can be acquired without effort, experience cannot. Money comes and goes, but experience, once you gain it, is with you forever. Now, that's something you can take to the bank.

22. In today's knowledge economy, most of your value is inside your head. That means whatever you learn in one job, you can take with you when you move on. If I were just starting out today, I would take advantage of this fact by looking for positions that would develop my technical skills. My advice is to work hard and acquire as much knowledge and experience as you can, so when opportunity knocks, you will be ready for it.

23. When you have a good idea, act on it. An ounce of *doing* is worth 10 pounds of *planning*. It is my belief that most people

will learn more and get closer to their goals by taking action and learning what works and what doesn't work for them.

24. Just as trying to accomplish too much can lead to exhaustion and burnout, setting your goals too low can lead to complacency, meandering and loss of interest. If we do not have to reach and go beyond what we believe we are capable of, there is no sense of accomplishment and no growth as a result of our success. No one rises to low expectations.

25. Leaders with a bold approach usually build far higher morale than those with a defensive outlook. They actively encourage their people to use their initiative and "give it a go." They expect and accept failures, but don't reward those who do nothing and never risk failing.

CHAPTER 13

THE ART OF GIVING BACK

"If you don't need it, give it away."
– Joe Segal

It has been said of Joseph Segal – if there is a good and noble cause, he is there. Together with his wife Rosalie, Joe has been deeply involved with and made significant contributions to the Jewish community and Simon Fraser University, as well as generous donations to the Variety Club, the United Way, B.C. Children's Hospital, Vancouver General Hospital and literally hundreds of other organizations. This generosity has been recognized with the Order of Canada, the Order of B.C. and the 2005 Variety Club International Humanitarian Award, to name but a few.

Joe is undoubtedly a self-made man and an entrepreneur who has never forgotten others. He maintains an open door to people from all walks of life and his family's selfless generosity is well known throughout the community.

Of all the men and women I have known in the Vancouver community, Joe and Rosalie intrigue me the most. Perhaps in part because despite all of the success they have achieved, neither of them has lost the sense of humility that perhaps stems from the fact that Joe came from a small farming community and never received a university education, or that Rosalie, at the age of 11, worked in her family's butcher shop in Chinatown, where she got up at 5 a.m.

each day to put on heavy boots and lug around hindquarters of beef, no matter how cold or hot the weather.

Joe is truly fortunate to have found his equal and the love of his life in his wonderful wife Rosalie, who could give any high-end hotel lessons in catering. Over the years, she has organized and hosted dozens of large-scale fundraising dinners at their home and Rosalie's attention to detail is legendary. She does it all – from the selection of invitations to valet parking for her guests, the entire evening is under her watchful eye and she always brings it off with such poise and grace.

Joe and Rosalie truly are friends of humankind and together, they make a formidable team. Together, they help and serve the community that we all live in, and it is a better place because of them.

There are numerous organizations that have benefited from Joe and Rosalie's generosity and the dinners they are famous for hosting, including:

Variety – The Children's Charity
Vancouver Symphony Orchestra
B.C. Children's Hospital
St. John Ambulance
David Foster Foundation
Canadian Red Cross
York House School
Jewish National Fund

The purpose of these dinners is always to raise money and

awareness for important causes and it's almost impossible to count up just how many millions of dollars have been raised for so many worthwhile organizations in our community. During just one dinner on behalf of Christ Church Cathedral, Joe and Rosalie were the catalyst for raising $2 million.

At the end of the day, our legacy in this life will be how many people we've helped and how well we've left this world after we've gone from it. Joe and Rosalie will be way up there on top of the list as those who set the standard for each of us in terms of generosity and citizenship.

As the embodiment of a fearless entrepreneur, Joe Segal has shown extraordinary vision and generosity in ensuring that others within the community have the opportunity to pursue their own dreams. We need look no further than Simon Fraser University for a perfect example.

In the 1980s, it was Joe who convinced the Simon Fraser University board to bring the university down from Burnaby Mountain to the downtown Vancouver community.

"SFU was the best-kept secret up on the hill, but if you wanted to be acknowledged by the business community, you needed a presence," explains Joe, who played an instrumental role in establishing the university's Harbour Centre campus downtown. The project is a unique example of cooperation between the corporate sector and an educational institution. It's also a testament to Joe's tenacity and his negotiating talents. In the end, the university came away with an outstanding downtown campus, virtually rent-free for 30 years.

In total, Joe served for more than 12 years on the Simon Fraser University board and was Chancellor of the university for six years. He also chaired the capital campaign for the creation of the Morris J. Wosk Centre for Dialogue at SFU and as mentioned in an earlier chapter, the Segal family donated the stunning heritage building that today houses the Simon Fraser University Segal Graduate School of Business. The building, which has been a landmark in Vancouver for more than 100 years, hosts all of SFU's MBA programs, as well as an MSc in Finance and a PhD program.

It's not surprising that Joe is proud of the city he has helped to shape. According to Joe, Vancouver is the greatest city in the world. It's also not surprising that the community he loves, loves him right back. Anyone who has read Peter Newman's book, *Titans: How the New Canadian Establishment Seized Power*, will likely remember the author's description of Joe: "When he lunches at the Four Seasons, which he does just about every day, he is greeted with genuine affection. He has done business with just about everybody in the room and even when he gets the best of the deal, no one resents Joe or asks for a recount. They trust his integrity. Joe always takes the time to hand out good advice and make significant donations to worthwhile causes. If the local Titans ever held a popularity contest, Joe Segal would win hands down."

"Make some money, use some money, give some money," that's Joe's approach to life and it's one that has served him well.

During our BCBusiness Top 100 Luncheon interview, I say

to Joe, "You have been honoured – from the Order of Canada and the Order of British Columbia to the Queen Elizabeth II Diamond Jubilee Medal – there probably isn't an organization that hasn't recognized you for the work that you and Rosalie have done. Is there one that really stands out as being the most important to you?"

"They're all important," Joe replies. "But sometimes the smaller the organization, the more important it is because you know there are so many needs out there that get bypassed and it's not the big, organized charities that you have to worry about not getting what they need. It's the small organization that is trying to fill a small niche within the community – one that no one else even knows exists – and they have nowhere to turn, those organizations are important. Sometimes $1,000 makes the difference and sometimes $200 and sometimes $5,000. It goes back to what I've said all along about giving, 'If you have a lot, a little means nothing. But if you only have a little, a little means a lot.' Life is simple, we complicate it."

Joe's philosophy has always been, "If I don't need it, why shouldn't someone else have it?" As someone who gets at least 15 to 20 requests a month from people who approach him out of the blue for help because they can't pay the mortgage or they've lost their job, Joe finds it easier to say yes than to say no.

"I don't say yes totally out of charity," explains Joe. "You know, if I'm not going to miss the money and I said no, I would go home and it would bother me. Money is to be used. If you take your money and you put it under the mattress or you put it in the bank, what does it do? Nothing. You don't see the pleasure and you don't derive any pleasure, what's the point of that? Part of the reason I give money away is because I'm a little selfish."

The president of High Point University, Nido Qubein, once told me that when we talk of philanthropy, we talk about money. But that's really not what philanthropy is about. It is more about the goodness of one's heart, the love in one's soul and the desire for a human being to leave this world a better place than he or she may have found it.

In fact, the word philanthropy comes from the Greek origin of two words. *Philos,* which means friend, and *anthropy,* which means humankind. So, a philanthropist then by definition would be a friend of humankind.

Joe is certainly that, as is Rosalie.

Of recent note is Joe's contribution to Vancouver General Hospital (VGH) and its mental health unit (he made a record-setting $12-million donation for a new building for the unit in 2010) and the story behind how the gift came about is as interesting as the contribution itself. In May of 2010, Joe had a stroke and ended up in Vancouver General Hospital for almost two weeks while he was recovering.

"I saw so much during those 12 days and our health-care system does a lot, but we can't leave it all up to the government to do, there's only so much money available," says Joe about his experience in the hospital. After asking around, Joe learned from various VGH staff that the most neglected department within the hospital was the mental health unit. In fact, the existing building was in such a state that a completely new building was really the only option.

"Cancer, heart disease, these are the causes that everybody is aware of because everyone has had exposure to those diseases," explains Joe. "I don't want to just support what's popular, I want to help where it is needed the most. Mental illness is kind of out of sight and there's a tendency to sweep it under the carpet because it makes many people uncomfortable. But mental illness crosses all boundaries; it doesn't just affect people on the Downtown Eastside. It also affects many professional people who suffer from stress-related mental health issues, young people who are prone to anxiety or depression and everyone in between. And the fact is, not only does mental illness affect the person who has the disease; it also impacts friends, family members, businesses and the community as well."

Initial estimates for the new mental health centre show that it is expected to cost about $73 million, with the province of B.C. contributing $48 million, while the VGH & UBC Hospital Foundation and a number of other corporate and private donors have committed $25 million.

"Rosalie and I are pleased that plans for the centre are now moving ahead," says Joe. "Our province needs this and we're happy we can help."

During one of our lunches after he had recovered from his

stroke, I ask Joe, "So why $12 million and not $10 million or even $15 million?"

"I just thought it was reasonable," replies Joe matter of factly. "I was there for 12 days and during that time they gave me back my health and so I figure a million dollars for every day is a fair trade."

CHAPTER 14

NO ORDINARY JOE

"If you want chicken soup,
you've got to put a chicken in the pot."
— Joe Segal

"Joe commands every encounter," says Aaron Fineman, president of Realty Concepts Inc., when I ask him to share some thoughts about Joe for this book. "Joe can find value in everything and his breadth of knowledge is astounding. Joe Segal really is one of a kind and he takes a genuine interest in what is going on around him. More often than not he begins and ends his conversations with the question, 'What else?' Joe has an irrepressible desire for knowledge."

"It is a tall order to write a few words that are truly descriptive of Joe Segal," says Aaron, who came from Winnipeg to work with Joe at Kingswood Capital more than a decade ago. "I think it is probably more fitting to use the words of others who are far more eloquent than myself and share some quotes that I believe capture the qualities and essence of a man who – I am quite certain everyone will agree – is no ordinary Joe."

Here then, with the assistance of some very wise individuals, are Aaron's thoughts on Joe Segal:

"Play the game for more than you can afford to lose . . . only then will you learn the game." – Winston Churchill

"Joe loves to tell the story of how he lost all of his hard-earned money at the age of 17 playing poker and ended up enlisting in the army and joining the Calgary Highlanders as a means to make his own way in the world," says Aaron. "It speaks volumes about his character that he didn't blame anyone else for his troubles or shirk responsibility for his actions. That was a turning point for Joe and he learned a valuable life lesson from that experience about taking risks. As a result, he is one of the most disciplined people I have ever encountered."

"Nine out of 10 businesses fail; so I came up with a foolproof plan: create 10 businesses." – Unknown

"As Joe will tell you himself, not everything he did was wildly successful," says Aaron. "But he has always been the kind of guy who turned things around and made the best of a situation. One year, when he still had his Fields clothing stores, he ordered a big shipment of bellbottom jeans for the upcoming summer season, but by the time they arrived, the style had changed to more of a straight-cut leg. Not one to be caught out by fashion trends, Joe cut the legs off the pants, turning them into cutoff shorts that sold for more than the bellbottoms would have."

"We make a living by what we get. We make a life by what we give." – Winston Churchill

"Joe spends so much of his time giving to others and puts so much thought into finding ways to help," explains Aaron. "He is genuinely troubled by people's stories and he gets letters all the time from individuals he's never met asking for his help. There is no way in the world that he could know if all of these requests are legitimate, but he still listens to every story because he worries that if he doesn't, someone will be left suffering when he could have made a difference. Anyone who calls on Joe gets a personal response, most of the time within 24 hours, and it would be very hard to find a situation where Joe says no to someone in genuine need."

"We are what we repeatedly do. Excellence, then, is not an act, but a habit." – Aristotle

"Joe Segal never does things halfway," according to Aaron. "Joe doesn't want to leave anything unexplored. Joe has a thirst for knowledge, he is interested in all things and, amazingly, he has full retention of everything. If you told him something 10 years ago, he could repeat back to you exactly what you said. If he's read something, he can recall every detail. Years ago, we were having lunch at the Four Seasons and at that time, when you walked out of the hotel, you could go right into the second floor of Holt Renfrew where there was a fur salon. As we walked through, Joe named off for me what each pelt was and where it was from; it was astounding. As we moved along the aisles, we noticed that the salesperson was following along, listening to what Joe had to say and it was clear that he was also learning something new. Over the years, I've come to realize that Joe has educated himself on a diverse array of subjects; he knows more about diamonds than a gemologist, more about sterling silver than Sheffields, more about flowers than a horticulturist and more about accounting than an accountant. It's remarkable."

"We can complain because rose bushes have thorns, or rejoice because thorn bushes have roses." — Abraham Lincoln

"Joe is the kind of guy who finds the good in everything. For that reason, Joe is someone that others seek out and enjoy spending time with," says Aaron. "When I first arrived in Vancouver to work on a project for Kingswood Capital, I had no idea who Joe Segal was. I was going to have lunch with him and everyone I talked to seemed to be in awe of the guy. I didn't understand what all the fuss was about. I didn't know Joe, but it didn't take long for me to understand."

"Management is doing things right. Leadership is doing the right things." — Peter Drucker

"More than anyone I have ever met, Joe is selfless in sharing his knowledge and experience with others," says Aaron. "When he walks into a room, everyone pays attention, not because he built a business empire or because he is a wealthy man, but because he treats everyone with respect and dignity. When my wife and I arrived in Vancouver, we knew few people and Joe and Rosalie welcomed us as if we were part of their family. I soon learned that working with Joe Segal was like having a Nexus pass, a diplomatic passport to the city. People trust his judgment and his circle of relationships is so vast, it's hard to find someone whose life he hasn't impacted."

"Distinction is the consequence, never the object, of a great mind." — Washington Allston

"I've worked with many people over the years and spent time with several titans of industry," says Aaron. "Joe Segal is different from everyone I've met. His ability to apply his knowledge is as amazing as the knowledge itself and he always presents himself in the most humble way imaginable. Joe is never too tired or too busy to ask, 'What else?' I have no doubt it is that ability to focus his attention like a laser and analyze every deal with a precision that others can only marvel at, that has made Joe Segal one of the most successful entrepreneurs in Canada and also one of the most sought-after mentors."

"Don't marry the person you can live with; marry only the person you can't live without." — James Dobson

"Joe is a man who has definitely got his priorities straight, as evidenced by a long and happy marriage of 64 years and counting," says Aaron. "Anyone who has met Joe knows that Rosalie is, and always has been, the woman he couldn't live without, from the first moment he laid eyes on her. During the many lunches we have shared over the past decade, Rosalie's name comes up frequently in conversation and when it does, Joe is not shy to admit that Rosalie is the most important thing in Joe's life. 'No one is invincible,' Joe will say. 'You're a hero today, you could be a bum tomorrow, but no matter what, when all the chips are down, if you're happily married, there's one person who will stand with you and that's all you need.'"

"You must be the change you wish to see in the world." – Mahatma Gandhi

"One evening, when Joe and Rosalie were driving in their car, headed out to a restaurant for dinner, Rosalie suddenly told Joe to stop the car," explains Aaron. "At the curb on Rosalie's side of the car was a man in a wheelchair, struggling to get down the street. Rosalie jumped out of the car and pushed the man in the wheelchair across the street and down the block to where he wanted to go and before leaving him, Rosalie also made sure that she left him with sufficient money for a few good meals. The extraordinary thing is that Joe and Rosalie are exactly alike in this regard; they both see things that others choose not to see and they both help those in need, regardless of whether it is convenient or comfortable to do so."

"You can't help getting older; but you don't have to get old." – George Burns

"Joe often says that he would trade all of his money to be 30 years old and broke, just to have the opportunity to do it all again," says Aaron with a smile. "Most people in their 30s don't have as much energy and enthusiasm for life as Joe does. He may be getting older, but as long as he continues to ask, 'What else?' Joe Segal will never get old."

CHAPTER 15

ROBERT D. CIMA

Regional Vice President & General Manager
Four Seasons Hotel Vancouver

There's not much that Mr. Segal and his family haven't celebrated at Four Seasons Hotel Vancouver – bar mitzvahs, bat mitzvahs, weddings, anniversaries, birthdays and fundraisers – not to mention the (literally) countless outside catering events at his home.

To quote Mr. Segal directly, he "is family akin to being furniture around here" and we couldn't agree more. He is as much a part of the family as is any staff member – having had a presence here longer than any current member of management.

After decades of his lunching with us every day at Chartwell, we brought him the blueprints when planning our new restaurant, Yew, to ask him where he wanted his regular table to be! Mr. Segal puts the power into "power lunch" and guests have been known to make reservations in Chartwell, and now Yew, in hopes of "accidentally" running into him. Not one to hold back his opinion, Mr. Segal has been the catalyst to menu rewrites, given his regular, honest feedback.

Four Seasons Vancouver has been the beneficiary of an impressive number of fundraisers and business meetings because guests knew that Mr. Segal would approve of the venue, and perhaps more importantly, because it would make it easy for him to attend, as chances are, he was already here.

Described by the staff who know him well, Mr. Segal is humble, generous, gentle and kind. The loyalty he has demonstrated to Four Seasons, Chartwell and Yew over the decades is legendary. He is one of our own and we wouldn't have it any other way. An extraordinary life indeed!

CHAPTER 16

DIANNE WATTS

Mayor, City of Surrey

Joe has had an extraordinary impact on B.C.'s business and philanthropic community. His leadership has inspired countless people and set an example that many of us have tried to emulate. His courage, generosity and positivity have had a great influence on so many people. He is a role model and mentor, and he has taught us all to take risks, live in the present, look to the future and be bold.

Over the years, I have watched Joe and Rosalie give back to their community in many impressive ways – supporting mental health projects, education endeavours and numerous other initiatives. Joe should be very proud of his family, as they too are such strong community leaders.

Joe is a legend in and out of the boardroom, and our country would benefit from having more leaders like Joe Segal.

CHAPTER 17

PAUL WONG C.M., BCom

Past President, Vancouver Chinatown Lions Club

Joe Segal gave me the following advice, which started my road to success. He said, "He who is not courageous enough to take risk will not accomplish anything in life."

My father emigrated to Canada from China at a very tender age. Because he does not speak English, he could not find a job. In order to survive, he opened a one-man hand laundry called Keefer Laundry. It was a miracle that he was able to bring his wife to Vancouver to raise six children. It is Chinese tradition for the oldest son in the family to carry on the family business.

At UBC, I wrote my graduation thesis on, "How I was going to build the biggest and most modern laundry in Canada." My professor did not believe me and just gave me a passing mark. After graduation, I took a big risk and I obtained a long-term loan from the Industrial Development Bank to build my new laundry. With the new facility, I was able to build my business by providing my customers with better service than my competitors. I invited my professor to the grand opening of the new laundry. I also informed him that my newest customer was UBC. He then apologized for underestimating my ability.

Joe Segal also advised me to give back to the community when

I became successful. He quoted Winston Churchill when he said, "We make a living by what we get, but we make life by what we give. You will never go broke by helping people."

When my father and sister passed away from cancer, I made a commitment to them that I would do something to eradicate cancer. I instigated the Medal of Merit Award for the Vancouver Chinatown Lions Club to raise funds for the BC Cancer Foundation. The Medal of Merit is the highest award given by Lions Clubs to a non-Lion who has made a big contribution to the community. Of the 10 Medal of Merit Award dinners that benefited the BC Cancer Foundation, the one honouring Joe and Rose Segal was the most successful. A total of $150,000 was raised, which included a donation of $25,000 from Joe Segal and a matching grant of $75,000 from Lions Club International Foundation. It was most gratifying that the research equipment that we purchased from the proceeds made a breakthrough in ovarian cancer research.

CHAPTER 18

JOHN D.L. MACKAY

CEO, Strand Corporation

One of the most meaningful and important events in the early years of my career was when I met Joe Segal. However, that day in the early 1970s actually did not come for more than six months after I first heard the name Joe Segal – then described to me as "one of the most successful young businessmen in Vancouver."

At that time I was attending university and running my painting contracting business. When I contacted the father of a friend who owned a building in downtown Vancouver that needed painting, he told me that the building had recently been sold to a Mr. Joe Segal. He then told me about this guy, Joe, who was not only smart and very successful, but also very generous: Joe had just given my friend's father a $10,000 "on the spot – without hesitation" charitable donation.

I thought to myself, 'This guy I have to meet! And I want the contract to paint his downtown warehouse building.' But getting to him wasn't easy. I was given Mr. Segal's office telephone number, and when I called I was put through to a nice lady named Alice. After three more calls, Alice suggested that, because Mr. Segal was so busy, I should write a letter of introduction regarding myself and my painting business. I thought, I was busy too – painting, not writing letters. Even though I didn't need another painting job at that time, I was now even more intent on meeting this "important guy." So I wrote the letter.

A few months later, an existing customer told me that one of his neighbours, named Mr. Segal, wanted to see me at his house on Hudson Street. I knocked on the Segal residence door and after I introduced myself to Mr. Segal, he said, "You sent me a letter a few months ago." We then walked around the house, I gave a quote for the exterior painting, and he immediately accepted. I then said that I was surprised that he remembered that I had sent the letter – to which he replied, only half-jokingly, I'm sure: "What do you mean you are surprised, I make it my business to know what goes on around this town; why the h--- do you think I'm so successful anyway?" We had a laugh together and our lifelong friendship began at that moment. As I drove away, I realized that Joe wasn't joking with that comment, and I took it deeply to heart, as I have with everything Joe has said to me since that day.

We instantly "connected" and from then on enjoyed a wonderful relationship. For some reason, I felt that I could always count on Joe to be there for me as a mentor and a friend. Just knowing that his support was in the background for me, gave me invaluable confidence in the early years of my career.

From that first small painting contract, Joe entrusted me with major jobs that showed his confidence in me, including downtown buildings and the exterior of the then-recently purchased Segal residence, Rio Vista, on Southwest Marine Drive. One of the most interesting requests from Joe was to clean his Honest Joe's building at a corner on Hastings Street, commonly known as Pigeon Square, and to do whatever was necessary to stop the pigeons from sitting on his building.

The moments that I had with Joe, either meeting or by telephone, were very special to me, and would always leave me a bit wiser and encouraged by his positive energy and support. As busy as he was, he always seemed to have time to take a personal interest in me and my future.

As I then embarked on the next stage of my business career in my mid-20s (post-university/post-painting company), I would look to Joe's success as an example and as an encouragement, for the potential of my own success. He showed me possibilities and windows of opportunity that I didn't know existed. He showed me how he invested in people first – that while each deal was important, the true art of the deal involved putting people first – as he had shown through his trust in me.

As time passed, although we never did any further business together, our friendship (and for me, the mentorship) continued, with Joe often encouraging me to follow his example of "giving back" to our community.

While space in this chapter doesn't permit me to share my many other "Joe Segal experiences," the essence of my friendship with Joe has been to provide me with the wisdom of many important life lessons – lessons that I still find invaluable in my life today.

CHAPTER 19

DOUG DIXON

Property Manager, Alexander Centre Management

I consider myself exceedingly fortunate to have worked for Joe Segal for 26 years and counting. I know him well and hold him in the highest possible esteem. Those who also know him well will no doubt agree with the following Joe Segal observations:

He is highly intelligent and very knowledgeable. He has the memory of an elephant and soaks up and retains information from many different sources.

Joe Segal is extremely generous, both with his time and his money. In addition to the philanthropy most know about, he gives money to everyone on the street who asks for it, just in case they really do need it, and more often than not will respond to unsolicited requests for help. Much to their credit, the Segals raised their children to be similarly generous.

Joe Segal is simply amazing in a meeting – entertaining, courteous, charming and disarming, but also a good listener. He always examines things from the other party's perspective and works towards a win-win situation. He tends to be fair bordering on overly fair and usually is happy to leave a little money on the table.

Joe Segal is loyal to those who are loyal to him. His

relationships tend to be very long and he takes care of people. He remembers what you did for him yesterday. You will never go wrong being Joe Segal's partner, friend or employee.

Joe Segal sees the big picture better than almost anyone else.

Joe Segal is perhaps the luckiest man I know. I think he would agree with me wholeheartedly on this.

When I say that Joe Segal is lucky, I do not mean to infer that his success has much, if anything, to do with luck. I have no doubt that he would be just as successful in any era and under almost any circumstances. The last meeting I attended in his office, he shared some fascinating stories about when he started out in business selling Second World War surplus goods that no one else could envision a use for. True to form, he could see what others did not and he seized the opportunity. He has done this countless times since. At the end of our meeting, he expressed that he would gladly give it all away to trade places with any of the other somewhat younger people in the room. Wouldn't it be something to witness what he would accomplish in round two?

Speaking of luck, I was hired by Joe Segal in 1986 largely by fluke via one of his Toronto partners who owned half of the Vancouver Show Mart building at the time. I had no idea who he was or what he was like. I have learned so much about real estate, and even more about people, from him over the years. Other than my family, this is literally the best thing that has ever happened to me.

CHAPTER 20

A. JOHN ELLIS O.C., LL.D. (Hon), O.R.S.

Honorary Director, Bank of Montreal
Governor, Canadian Chamber of Commerce
Chairman Emeritus, Canada Development Corporation (CDC)

Joe, whose business and philanthropic activities are of the highest order, is one of the most remarkable persons I have ever known in my going on 99 years. Modest but very successful in everything he does, he has been an inspiration to witness.

Many years ago, I was his banker when it was quite apparent to me that he was a "self starter" who required very little monetary advice – a deal maker par excellence. But there are many other sides to his psyche: a dedicated family man, a strong community-minded person and a proud Canadian who believes in democratic values. For example, he voluntarily and actively fought for international freedom during the Second World War enduring the hardships of the battles in Northwest Europe as an infantryman. Like the rest of us, he anxiously awaited repatriation after VE Day to get back to Canadian business and community activities.

Among his many accomplishments, one that stands out in my mind was his appointment as Chancellor of Simon Fraser University, which has become an internationally and highly regarded institution after a rather shaky start in the mid '60s. Joe was very much a part of its success. His unfailing good advice was greatly appreciated and followed by the senior staff, as I know from discussions with them.

I have had the pleasure of meeting with Joe both socially and businesswise since the mid '60s, and one little never-to-be-forgotten episode proves that he by nature is a magnanimous person. This was proven to me one day when we were both on the same flight from Vancouver to Toronto for business reasons. On arrival we travelled by limousine together to downtown Toronto where Joe was the first to disembark in front of his hotel, where the driver reached into the trunk and handed *my* briefcase to Joe. We then proceeded to the Central Railway station where I checked *Joe's* briefcase, not noticing it was not mine. After business meetings at my Toronto office, I was scheduled to take the Via Rail overnight trip to Montreal for further meetings. Fortunately I had mentioned to Joe about the Via Rail trip that evening. When I arrived rather late that evening at the station, I was surprised to find Joe pacing up and down awaiting my arrival – and his briefcase! Instead of being extremely annoyed, as he had every right to be, he just laughed it off. We continued to laugh later on over lunch in Vancouver.

CHAPTER 21

PATRICK OSWALD

Leadership Giving, United Way; Leadership Giving, The Nature Trust of B.C.

HILARY OSWALD

Co-founder, Pacific Riding for Developing Abilities

Making our community of the Lower Mainland a far better place for us all is a talent Joe and Rosalie share in abundance.

We have been blessed with helping to start two United Way Agencies – the Western Institute for the Deaf, and Pacific Riding for Developing Abilities. Therefore it was appropriate that Patrick endeavour to build United Way's "Leadership Giving." Having created $1,000 donors named Leaders of the Way and Leaders of the Future (those who tuck United Way into their wills), Patrick decided to "up the ask" in 1986 and create Patrons – $5,000-a-year donors.

"Chunky" N. Woodward, Mrs. Gordon Southam, Frank A. Griffiths and Peter W.N. Graham all suggested that Joe Segal should be asked to join them in co-signing a letter to encourage others to give $5,000.

"Come and get my signature!" was the response from Joe. Thus, a delightful new chapter embellished Patrick's life.

Although in 1985, the United Way of the Lower Mainland

raised $10.2 million, this was not sufficient to completely fund its 86 agencies' needs. It also prevented encompassing many other human care agencies from joining the United Way, and so benefiting from the annual campaign.

Joe came to the rescue. "You are not asking me for enough money! Rosalie can host over 60 people in our home Rio Vista on Southwest Marine Drive. Invite all who give $2,500 and up, and we will get them to give $10,000, and so bring more human care agencies into the United Way campaign," exhorted Joe with enthusiasm. "Splendid!" replied Patrick, "but Joe, what shall we call these $10,000 annual donors?"

Joe, who had been in the Calgary Highlanders during the Second World War, pondered the question. "In the war we had those Pathfinder planes that led the way... so call us Pathfinders!" exclaimed Joe.

The famous Pathfinders Annual Dinners became a reality. The first dinner was held in Joe and Rosalie's own home, then the Prow Restaurant, followed every year since by Pathfinders Dinners held at the Four Seasons Hotel with over 200 donors in attendance.

On the 25th-anniversary Pathfinders Dinner honouring Joe and Rosalie in particular, as the dinner's founders, Patrick was privileged to read a poem thanking Joe and Rosalie for having created such a huge philanthropic example, benefiting all who are so fortunate to live in the same city as Joe and Rosalie.

Yes, indeed, on meeting Joe and Rosalie, a truly delightful chapter in one's life opens up!

CHAPTER 22

NORMAN PAUL BScPh

President, AAPharma Inc.
CEO, Next Paradigm Solutions

Robinson Ogilvy was deal No. 4. This is one of my favourite stories about Joe and me. We were having a great dinner with wine followed by some wonderful cognac at Maxwell's Restaurant in Hamilton. After the meal, Joe turns to me and says, "Lucky, I'm going to tell you the three most important secrets in business and life." At this point, I strain to clear my head for what was about to be the pinnacle of my Master Class with Joe. He then proceeds to explain that first and foremost, always know where the other guy is at. I think that's useful, but No. 2 has to be better. "If you can't fix it, then leave it. Only concentrate on what you can change." He's about to move onto the third and last bit of advice. "Lucky, this is everything!" Before he can say another word, our waiter interrupts Joe to ask him if he wants another glass of XO. I tell the waiter to disappear because Joe is about to divulge No. 3! Joe pauses, then looks to me and says, "What the hell was I talking about?" I repeat our entire conversation to him, up to and including his second secret in business and in life. He couldn't remember what he was thinking about, so we call it a night. Over breakfast at the Royal Connaught Hotel the next morning, I repeat the entire conversation from the night before. Still no No. 3. To this day, whenever I visit Joe, I ask him about No. 3. We both have a great laugh!

The last time I had lunch with Joe was at the Four Seasons in Vancouver. Joe went to the men's room and on his way back, he picked up two glasses of wine that the manager gave to him from a wine tasting of Argentinian Malbecs being held in an adjoining area. Shortly afterwards the hotel manager and the owner of the bar came over to our table to ask Joe what he thought of the wines. Joe said, "Gentlemen, the wine is wonderful but you cannot get more than $29.95 for a Malbec. At $100 a bottle, it won't sell." The owner of the bar explained to Joe about his costs and Joe simply said, "Forget the cost, it's what the market will pay that counts!" Joe then turned to me and asked if I was happy. "Yes, very happy," I answered, to which he replied, "Lucky, I will make you a deal. I'll trade all my wealth for your age." This is the only deal I couldn't complete with Joe. I love the fact that I am 68 and he still considers me to be young. In Joe's world, I still have "some runway" left. As for my nickname, he was absolutely right. I have been very lucky to have been able to share all these great times with Joe. I did consider a counter-proposal to Joe's Offer on the age-for-wealth swap, which was meeting him halfway, so we would be about the same age, and then for a brief moment imagined many more great lunches/dinners with Joe.

CHAPTER 23

WENDY LISOGAR-COCCHIA LL.D. (Hon)

CEO, Century Plaza Hotel/Absolute Spa Group

Joe put down the menu quickly, almost defiantly, and said in an uncompromising voice, "I don't feel like anything here today, I'm in the mood for a burger."

As I immediately pushed back my chair to get up, pondering to myself exactly where Mr. Segal would choose to go for Vancouver's finest burger, he directed me to sit down.

"Where are you going?" he asked with a perplexed look on his face.

"I don't see a burger on the Four Seasons menu," I replied, looking more than a little confused myself.

With a massive twinkle in his eye and a smile that was absolutely beyond charming, he leaned across the table and whispered to me, "Oh, they'll make us one."

For over a decade now, I have considered myself one of the most fortunate people in the world to call Joe a friend, mentor and father figure. My dad, Roy Lisogar, and Joe both came from the same small town in Alberta. Most people haven't heard of Vegreville, which is located east of Edmonton and with a population of just under 6,000 people, that's not surprising. But what is amazing to me is that these two incredible men, both of whom have had the most tremendous influence on my life, are from there.

Joe and my dad didn't just share a common birthplace, they also have many shared personality traits that played an important part in making them both legendary figures. First and foremost of those traits would be their deep love for, and prioritization of, family. There hasn't been one lunch with Joe or one chat that I recall having with my father where they didn't speak of their wives in the first few sentences. Their "better half" as both of them would affectionately refer to the women in their lives.

"Are you keeping your hubby Sergio happy?" Joe often asks of me over lunch.

I retaliate with a grin, "You know, Joe, the real question is, is Sergio keeping me happy?"

If there's one lesson that Joe has reiterated enough times that I can hear it in my head, it's this: "If everything is good at home and your spouse and children are happy and healthy, then you can start you day and concentrate on earning a living."

Having lost my own father far too soon, Joe has graciously stepped into the role and in the time between our lunches, I often yearn to hear Joe's voice and watch his mannerisms, the similarities with my father are uncanny and in some ways it makes me feel closer to him.

I marvel at how much they shared in common; the tenacious work ethic, the strong determination to succeed, the courage to blaze new trails and an unwavering commitment to community;

two self-made men and two legendary success stories.

One day over lunch, Joe asked me how my new spa chain was flourishing. In Joe terms, that translates to numbers. Now I was taught early on by my mother and father never, ever, under any circumstances, does one disclose their gross revenue, let alone their net.

When I told him I couldn't possibly disclose those details, Joe simply smiled and that's when I discovered how much he loves to estimate a company's financial status.

"Let me guess," he said. "You are grossing this much, your margin is that and you are netting this much."

"Well, Joe," I replied, "that's not much of a guess because it's absolutely bang on! How on earth did you do that?"

He smiled back at me and look around the restaurant's dining room.

"Pick any person in this room and if I know them, I can do it again," he told me.

And of course he did, again and again and again.

Anther one of a million things I love about Joe is that he is a man of his word, a handshake-deal kind of guy whose word is as good as any legal contract. I remember asking for his advice about adding a new location to the spa chain as we waited for our burgers that day we were having lunch at the Four Seasons, and he wisely advised me on the importance of trust.

"If you can't seal the deal on the shake and know you can trust them, why would you ever consider working with them?"

advised Joe.

Just at that moment, the hamburgers arrived and I was a little sad as I realized the fantastic lesson would come to an end as we munched on what turned out to be two amazing burgers. Of course, we've had many more lunches since that day, because the best thing about Joe is that he is one of the most unselfish people I have ever met, which means he always has time for a call, or a bit of fatherly advice . . . or even a burger.

From my family to yours, Joe, thank you for sharing your wisdom and love.

CHAPTER 24

ROBERT J. MACDONALD

President, Macdonald Development Corporation

I have been lucky to have a few mentors in my life who have had great effect on me. I became quite close to some of my mentors before they passed away and some mentors are still great friends. Some mentors you spend very little time with, but you get to know them by reading their biographies or hearing them speak.

I have not spent a great deal of time with Joe Segal. We are acquaintances, but I believe that both of us would call each other friends.

Joe is widely respected as we all know, but why is that? My observations are that Joe Segal is:

Caring and compassionate towards his fellow man;

Charismatic in the way he can converse with anyone and hold their interest;

Charitable and generous to a fault by giving and supporting others to help the community;

Dedicated to his family;

Energetic, persistent and hard working;

Fair, honest and reliable in his dealing of all types;

Experienced and intelligent;

Responsible;

Helpful;

Youthful; and

Friendly.

And I am sure that Joe has a longer list of positive qualities that I do not know about.

How fortunate our community is to have a man like Joe Segal around, and though he may not realize it, he is very inspirational and sets a tremendous example to anyone who wants to find a way to be a good person and have a meaningful life.

Joe Segal has been a very inspirational mentor to me, for which I am very grateful.

CHAPTER 25

LES BRADBURY

Sales, Marketing and Consulting

I joined Fields stores in the early '70s as a men's and boys' wear buyer following a successful interview with Mr. Segal and his vice president Fred Graves. My previous experience with the Hudson's Bay Company and Army & Navy stores seemed to work in my favour.

It was immediately evident that Fields Stores was a dynamic company in expansion mode. Some years earlier the company had bought a number of Bay stores, a division of small rural stores in places such as Williams Lake, Hope, Kimberley and Smithers.

Later I ran into Hugh Lorimer, the Hudson's Bay executive charged with disposing of this division. He had received a phone call from Joe Segal's office asking if he could come over to discuss the deal. He answered, "Yes, let's fix an appointment." "How about today?" came the reply, and an astonished Hugh Lorimer did just that! The whole deal was confirmed on a handshake with details and signings to be completed later.

The purchase of the Zellers chain took place while I was with Fields. It was top secret and only revealed to us when we were instructed, "JS wants everyone in the boardroom." It was a major coup. The transition meant continuous travel between Vancouver and Montreal for Mr. Segal and after one trip he asked Max Powel the merchandise manager and myself if we had worked with Triton Importers, and what we didn't buy from them. We had declined a boys' ski jacket, and it transpired "so had Zellers." Joe Segal told us, "because Triton's best price was too high. They're stuck with it. Offer them $6 [against their $8.50] and you might get it."

Joe Segal knew all the vendors that Zellers and Fields worked with and his outstanding retention for detail and number amazed us – once again. He is the most visionary, detailed, knowledgeable, strategic, perceptive businessman I've ever worked with. And we got the jacket.

My time at Fields was the best working period of my life. Although Joe criticized me (tongue in cheek) for one fault: "Les is okay, but these Englishmen just don't have a sense of humour!"

CHAPTER 26

PATRICK J. JULIAN

Partner, Koffman Kalef LLP, Business Lawyers

As a commercial real estate lawyer I was aware of the reputation of Joe Segal long before I met the man. In 1994 I joined the law firm of Koffman Kalef where Joe's good friend and legal advisor, Morley Koffman, Q.C., carried out work on behalf of Joe. I have been blessed by having the opportunity to act on behalf of Joe, his companies and his family on various real estate transactions and right from the beginning I was in awe of his command of the issues and his brilliant ability to carry out real estate valuation calculations in his head. No pen or paper on Joe's desk!

Even while I was a younger lawyer Joe treated me with respect and attention. He has a special sense of humour with me that is reserved for solicitor-client relationships! I always welcomed the opportunity to meet at Joe's office because I knew I was going to learn not just about the transaction that Joe was involved with, but receive lessons in life itself.

Joe has always been fair and reasonable in his business dealings. He said to me on a number of occasions that it was important to "leave a nickel on the table" for the other side. Do not grind to the point where you may get a slightly better financial deal, but you have lost something in terms of your humanity and who you are as a person. I believe that business people come back from time to time to deal with Joe on different transactions because they know he can be trusted and, in the end, although he will only enter into the transaction if it makes business sense to him, he will be fair.

I have had the privilege and honour of lunching with Joe both in the earlier days at Chartwell as well as at Yew at the Four Seasons. I admire the fact that his mind is alive and young and is always seeking information and transaction details, and he is always excited to debate the merits of a particular investment or development.

There is no one who wants to live and enjoy each day more than Joe. He has explained to various people his analysis of the "runway of life." Without going into the details of that philosophy it has led to a number of occasions where Joe has asked me my age and, with a twinkle in his eye, has suggested that he would trade half his fortune if we would trade ages. I note now that I am 60, those offers seem to be not forthcoming as much as they were 20 years ago!

As you practice law and provide legal advice to clients, you do over the years recognize people of character and personal values that draw you to them, not just for the purpose of giving legal advice but also because of your admiration of their personalities and successes. I would put Joe at the top of my all-time client list.

CHAPTER 27

BROOKE WADE FCA

President, Wade Capital Corporation

My mentor, Joe Segal, taught me many ways to look at giving. His simplest rule of generosity was if you won't miss it, give it away. But Joe went further than that and taught me something deeper – that a real gift is when you give something you can't be without. Many of us have heard Joe's story in which an old woman goes into her grocery jar for precious money to give a gift to someone in need and then crosses off a food item from her shopping list. Well, a special encounter with a Massai warrior helped me to understand what Joe had been trying to teach me – that a real gift cannot be replaced.

Our family had befriended a Massai warrior, "Wilson" Meikuaya, during a visit to the Free the Children outpost in Kenya. We were deeply privileged that Meikuaya was able to visit us at our home in Canada a few years later. The trip strengthened our friendship and fostered new memories of snow-covered mountaintops, Beluga whales and zodiac rides. At the end of the visit, as we prepared to say goodbye, it became clear that my friend was about to give me a gift. I had received many gifts in my life but little did I know that the next moment would completely change my definition of a gift.

Massai live a sparse lifestyle. They carry their trophies in the form of beautiful beaded chains and bands, each commemorating a special event in their life's journey. When Meikuaya presented me with his gift, he placed around my neck a beautiful three-stranded necklace. As he explained the meaning behind the necklace, it became clear that it was the same necklace his Mama had taken six months to craft to commemorate his graduation from university. It was such an extraordinary gesture that at first I tried to decline the gift and to convince him to carry it with him on my behalf. My efforts were of no avail.

At that moment, when the Warrior gave me something so precious to him that it could not possibly be replaced, I understood the lesson Joe had been trying to teach me.

I could almost hear Joe whispering in my ear: "Now there is a real gift."

CHAPTER 28

COLIN BOSA

CEO, Bosa Properties Inc.

Joe Segal taught me a wonderful lesson. In 2009, amidst the economic crisis, Joe calmly purchased the Grosvenor Building in downtown Vancouver. At the time there were few buyers doing deals, and many thought the real estate industry was headed for collapse just as he purchased this significant asset. Later, I had the opportunity to ask Joe Segal and Aaron Fineman about the acquisition, and when I posed the question, "What did you see that so many missed?" their answer was simple: "It is good real estate." Their answer reinforced something that I have long known but still fascinates me when I see it in action and that is, if you buy good assets at fair prices for the long term, you will do well.

I have always distinguished between intelligence and wisdom. As the world speeds up, and information comes at us faster and faster, we are losing that patient, simplistic wise approach to life. It seems to me that anyone can complicate life; it is actually more difficult to simplify life. Joe is a testament to that.

When I witness those like Joe who have chosen this path, a path of moral character, deep values and simplicity, it strikes me that they are always deeply peaceful and happy. And if you are not smiling along the way, then what is it for? My father has long said that true success doesn't come from just reaching the summit, but rather the lucky ones are those people who reach the summit and when standing on the top of the mountain, they look around and they see their friends and family at their side. As Joe stands on the summit looking back on a wonderful life, he stands there with all his friends and family, and they are many — and that is true success.

CHAPTER 29

GARRY ZLOTNIK FCA, BCom, CFP, CLU, ChFC

President, ZLC Financial Group

Our family has had the great pleasure of having many interactions with Joe. My father, who passed away in 2008, first met Joe when he came back from the Second World War and started selling life insurance. They had an instant connection and I believe they shared the same hard work ethic and the desire to succeed.

My brothers and I have all had opportunities to meet with, learn from and interact with Joe. These interactions revolved mostly around business, charity and politics.

I myself have had the opportunity to meet with Joe on numerous occasions regarding our business. The most striking and incredible attribute that has continually stood out to me is Joe's ability to instantly get to a financial solution in his head. My brother Mark and I are both CAs, and while we're stumbling around looking for calculators, Joe has always had the financial analysis at his fingertips.

A few years ago Mark was chair of a non-profit. He had to make a decision that involved staff as well as potential litigation. Joe, who was a major supporter of the non-profit, phoned Mark and gave him advice that helped resolve the issue. Essentially Joe's message was that it was more important to do the right thing than to be right. That message rings true in many situations.

We've learned a great deal from Joe. So when they say that imitation is the sincerest form of flattery, I can say with a clear conscience that I've "borrowed" the following quote from Joe before:

"The more you give, the more you get."

I have heard Joe say this on many occasions at charity events. It took awhile for me to really understand the meaning of this, especially early on in my career. It's not about some financial reward you're getting. The reality is, when you've achieved a certain level of success that makes you fortunate enough to be in a position to make a difference and you exercise that privilege, you're rewarded with an amazing sense of fulfillment and gratification. In addition, there is no question that it provides you with a certain level of respect and power. And, of course, giving both your time and your money is even more gratifying. As my brothers and I age, Joe's quote continues to provide us with meaning, because at the end of the day, these endeavours form part of our legacy.

CHAPTER 30

ART REITMAYER FCA, MBA

Past President & CEO, Rick Hansen Foundation
Past President & CEO, Channel M Television

In the course of my six-plus-year partnership with Joe at Channel M, I was fortunate to have many conversations with him where he shared a number of lessons and some of the wisdom he has accumulated from his years in business. Each came with a wonderful story that could make up a book all on its own. Following is a recap of just some of the highlights for me.

Luck plays a role in most successful businesses. Early on Joe purchased a large quantity of surplus lighter flints that fit a very specific high-end lighter. When he purchased the flints he felt there was little downside due to how little he paid, but the challenge was finding someone for whom they had greater value. Luck came in the form of a buyer wanting to make a knock-off brand that needed Joe's flints. Flints for which Joe paid $500 sold for $10,000, a return even beyond his expectation.

Always leave something on the table for the next guy . . . don't be greedy. When Joe was purchasing and selling surplus inventory from Sears in the early days of Fields, the individual who had made the arrangement could not pay for the product and Joe could have gone direct and cut him out of the deal and made a larger margin. Joe did pay direct but also paid 10 per cent to the individual who made the original arrangement. While not necessary, Joe felt it was important that he left something for the other guy and maintained longer-term relationships. This practice has continued throughout Joe's career and while no one would accuse him of being a soft negotiator, he is known for being fair and honourable.

Reinvest in your business and never live beyond your means — leave money in the business, don't bleed it. Joe's businesses were able to grow because he continually took money that he made and reinvested. While it forced him to grow his company organically, it also allowed him to always keep a substantial ownership stake.

Value is key to how a business if perceived. Don't sell cheap stuff cheap; sell good stuff cheap. The key for Joe was that in order to win at the game of business, you need to provide good value. Providing a low-quality product or poor service at a low price is not offering good value and will not create loyalty in the customer or a business advantage. The key is to offer more for less.

It is better to give with a warm hand than a cold one. Joe is legendary in Vancouver for his support of numerous community organizations and is fond of the saying that "you can't take it with you." So it is better to give what you can while you are alive rather than waiting and leaving it until you pass away. Joe is a strong believer in the need to support and give something back to the community in which you live, both through your business and personally.

Joe's business success began because he had an uncanny ability to sell, a sense of what the market would buy, a passion to succeed and the ability to work hard. Having lunch with Joe is better than reading any 10 how-to business books or spending hours in classroom study . . . it is always more than worth the price of admission.

CHAPTER 31

DAVID SIDOO

Executive Chairman, East West Petroleum

Growing up in the Vancouver area, I often read about Joe Segal in the newspapers. Whether it was a major business acquisition or a substantial donation to a charity, it was always front-page news (and still is). I never envisioned I would cross paths with Joe, let alone build a friendship with him and Rosalie. In the years that I have gotten to know Joe, he has always had the time whether he is busy or not to provide me with important insight. There are two great pieces of valuable advice that Joe has continuously shared with me in the way that only Joe can. On the home front: "A happy wife makes for a happy life." Looking at him and Rosalie, this is so true. In the business world, Joe, forever the visionary, has always said PLAN: whether it is building a house ("David, did you plan?") or altering a business venture ("David, did you plan?").

I am proud to call Joe Segal my friend, a titan who from very humble beginnings, through incredible hard work and implausible generosity, has given so much to be proud of. Mahatma Gandhi said it best: "In a gentle way, you can shake the world." Joe, with your gentle soul you truly have shaken the world, with all your professional accomplishments and personal generosity. You have set the standard for the next generation of proud Canadians to make a difference in their communities.

CHAPTER 32

ANDREW BIBBY

Chief Executive, Grosvenor Americas

I have followed Joe's long career in the retail trade and, particularly, in real estate. I first ran into him when we sold Kingswood Capital land (through his son Lorne) at Annacis Island, Grosvenor's long-term business-park holding in Vancouver. At the time, what struck me most about Joe was his reliance on intuition and his ability to simplify a deal to its most essential elements. I also first heard his now-familiar expression, "That seems fair," as he came around to accepting the negotiated terms.

One of our most interesting deals with Joe was when he bought our office building, the Grosvenor Building, in Vancouver.

As Joe always says, "There is a time to buy and a time to sell." And, in the case of the Grosvenor Building, his timing was impeccable. Jamie Delmotte, who managed the sale at Grosvenor, recounts the story best:

"During the summer of 2008, we decided to sell the Grosvenor Building into a very strong market and in early September agreed terms with an investor to sell the building at what would have been a record price for a Vancouver office building. As events unfolded and the financial markets collapsed in the fall of 2008, the sale fell through. In early 2009, our broker received a call from Joe, 'Kevin, will Grosvenor sell me their building?'

"Kevin responded, 'Joe, what's your number?'

"Joe answered, 'Let me think about it.'

"Several weeks later, after a lot of back and forth, it all came down to one final meeting. We put our number in front of Joe and said, 'Joe, if you want the building, here's our number and we need and unconditional offer.' Joe sat silent for a few minutes and then suggested we step out of his office and wait in the Yew Bar. Over the period of an hour, we took several calls from Joe and Gary as they tried to improve the deal. We stood our ground. Eventually, Joe asked us to return to his office. Joe opened with, 'Well, I suppose you want me to s--- or get off the pot.' Several minutes later the deal was done. In classic Joe style, he had the patience and vision to buy when no one else would.

"For Grosvenor, getting Joe to agree to an unconditional deal in such a volatile time was critical. Joe was comfortable taking that risk, as he knew the standards to which Grosvenor maintains its buildings. Several weeks later, one of the largest tenants in the building decided that they would be moving out of the building. Again, in classic Joe style, he didn't bat an eyelid and closed without issue."

The manner in which Joe approached this deal provided me with a lot of insight into why he is so successful: patience, courage, integrity and a nose for a good deal. In this case, he knew that it was the time to buy and, with the benefit of hindsight, he got a very, very fair deal.

CHAPTER 33

HARRY BLOY

MLA, Burnaby-Lougheed
Deputy Chair, Committee of the Whole
Special Liaison, International Business Opportunities

I have had the privilege and honour of knowing Joe Segal personally for 10 years, and by reputation for even longer. He is a remarkable self-made man whom I respect and admire very much. To say that I look up to him as a mentor would be an understatement.

Joe is someone who never brags about his wealth and never fails to ask about your family and how you are doing. He genuinely cares. And at 87 years of age, he still goes to work every day alongside his family members. In fact, it was the obvious caring and passion that Joe has for his family that really drew me to him and made me like and respect him so much.

I've also had the honour of having lunch with Joe on many occasions over the years. For those who know him, lunch with Joe at the Four Seasons Hotel is legendary in Vancouver because, as his guest, you are seen to be very special and he makes you his sole focus regardless of who else enters the room. He even has his own reserved table for these daily lunches. And if he does not like something you may have done, or a position you've taken on an issue, he will discuss it with you but will never force his opinion on you.

Joe's knowledge is not limited to the world of business. He also knows much about history and aboriginal art, and I believe he knows every flower in his garden. And if you ask Joe a question, he does not answer it directly but rather he will tell you a story.

Joe's generosity is also well known and he has given so much back to his community, to our province and to the country. Many organizations have benefited from his guidance as a board member and from his abilities as a fundraiser. But it is his ability to teach organizations and boards how to fundraise that is perhaps his most lasting gift to them.

I am grateful to Joe for the wisdom and direction he has given me in the business of government and in life, and I am pleased to have this opportunity to thank him and acknowledge him publicly. He is a generous friend and he has given so much more to me than I could ever possibly give back.

CHAPTER 34

DUNCAN K. DAVIES

President & CEO, International Forest Products Limited (Interfor)

Joe Segal joined Interfor's board of directors in 1987, as a favour, I expect, to the company's founder, Bill Sauder.

Joe and Bill were like-minded in many respects: self-made entrepreneurs, strong family men, active community supporters and philanthropists.

The fact that Bill's chosen field was primary resources, manufacturing and distribution and Joe's was retail and property development enabled them to work together on a number of business matters without competing with one another.

Bill served as Chair of the Board of Governors and Chancellor of UBC for many years; Joe did the same at SFU.

Bill and his family have given generously – and often anonymously – to numerous charitable causes and endowed the Sauder School of Business at UBC. Joe and his family have done the same, as well as endowing the Segal Graduate School of Business at SFU.

I often wondered if it was a competition between Bill and Joe to see who could do more for the community. I once watched the two of them work the crowd at a B.C. Children's Hospital fundraiser raising $1.2 million for the BCCH in the space of 30 minutes. I don't think the crowd knew what hit them that night.

At the end of the day, it doesn't really matter if they were competing with each other: the people of B.C. have been the beneficiaries of their generosity and will be for decades to come.

I first met Joe when I was asked by Bill to help him pull Interfor out of a tailspin in 1998. The Japanese lumber market had collapsed and Interfor was ill prepared to deal with the fallout. I knew Joe by reputation. My guess is he had no idea who I was and my sense is he was skeptical I was going to be able to help Bill deal with the challenges he was facing.

As it turned out, we were able to get Interfor back on track – largely due to Bill's focus and determination.

The company's board – including Joe –played an extremely important role during that period.

I don't believe Joe had any particular affection for the lumber industry. Nor did he bring technical expertise to the table.

What he brought, if anything, was even more valuable.

Joe has an inherent understanding of people and business that provided great context for our discussions and deliberations.

I learned to listen when Joe talked. Inevitably, there was a kernel of wisdom in his comments that was relevant to the issues we were dealing with. And, I like to think he concluded that I was up to the task after all.

Joe stayed with us until 2006, long enough to see Interfor embark on a new journey that we continue on today.

Unfortunately, we lost Bill in 2007.

And, while Joe is no longer active with Interfor, he's still going strong with his business interests and in the community and his family members are walking actively in his footsteps.

I hope Joe looks back fondly on his time with Interfor knowing he was a huge source of support for Bill, me and our company at a challenging time in our history.

CHAPTER 35

KEVIN BENT

Executive Vice-President, PostMedia Inc.
President & Publisher, The Vancouver Sun and The Province

I met Joe in the fall of 2006 at a fundraising event. I soon learned that it was not unusual for Joe and Rosalie to support many such business and charitable events. In fact, I became aware that they were among the most generous philanthropists in our community. After crossing paths a few times that fall, Joe casually mentioned we should have lunch one day soon.

The morning of the lunch I was excited and a little nervous as I was dining with one of Vancouver's most iconic entrepreneurs; matter of fact, one of Canada's most successful business leaders.

I remember my first lunch with Joe as if it were yesterday, not 2006. He immediately put me at ease, as he does in his way, and it was the first time I recognized this special talent. He asked me about my family, gave insights into his business and asked about my business. He shared with me that he read seven newspapers a day, including the two local dailies. He shared how he and Rosalie used newspapers to identify some of their next philanthropic endeavours, whether large or small. It was a great lunch. All of our lunches since then, for me, have been memorable.

He is a true humanitarian, someone who truly 'gets it.' I learned that you could be an accomplished business leader as well as a compassionate philanthropist.

Over the course of numerous lunches, I learned of his extensive business experience, witnessed his sharp wit and sense of humour and was keenly aware of his deep compassion for others.

His advice to me was often told as a story. He was direct, but he had a simple and extremely entertaining way of communicating complicated life lessons. On this particular day, Joe asked me, "Kevin, if I gave you a very large amount of money, what would you do with it?" I was speechless. He went on to say that he would be glad to give me all of his wealth if he could trade places and be my age again. This is a confident man who knew he could do it all over again. In fact, he'd welcome it. We talked through what he meant and since then I've often thought about his question. I've interpreted our discussion in many different ways over the years. Each meaning was profound and insightful. Joe in his way was saying, time is your most valuable commodity; don't waste it as it goes by quickly. He was also saying there is no better time than the present to pursue what makes you happy. I believe he was also saying that if you have a dream, chase it and never give up. The other piece of advice that has become an important mantra for me is to give back to our community. He said give your time – it's valuable, your expertise – it will make a difference, and give financially – until it hurts. There are people that need the help a lot more than you. I am always grateful to "Lunch With Joe."

CHAPTER 36

DERRAL G. MORIYAMA

Senior Vice-President, Business Development, Western Canada
BMO Bank of Montreal

In May of 2003, I was transferred to Vancouver from our headquarters in Toronto. This was a homecoming of sorts; my father had been born in the Fraser Canyon near Boston Bar and had lived in Vancouver before the Second World War. When our family assets were seized and the family moved inland, my father decided to move to Calgary and raise our family there. We had relatives in the Interior of B.C. and we visited Vancouver often.

My new role was senior vice-president, Vancouver, for Bank of Montreal, which included responsibilities for both retail and commercial banking. Part of my initial duties was to familiarize myself with the composition of our customer base, including identifying our top clients. Through my discussions with our team, one name stood out clearly as an influential client I should meet – a gentleman by the name of Joe Segal. As the story (and legend goes), Joe had been a top customer of the bank since the 1940s. When our CEOs came to town, Joe was on the list of people they had to meet with. His prowess at developing business, picking top real estate transactions and his philanthropy were considered second to none. Although not a part of the documents in the file (we have a tendency to cull older documentation), I understand we had worked with Joe on a proposal that would see him put an offer in to purchase the Hudson's Bay Company with our support. This was amongst the dozens of transactions we acted on as Joe's bankers. Joe's integrity was beyond reproach – his word truly was his bond. I was told of the many, many philanthropic initiatives he was involved with. I also heard of the countless times he helped out people – sometimes strangers – to show them a path, lend a hand, provide a personal loan that may or may not be repaid. He set up programs, co-signed loans and developed the path for people to climb out of tough situations and stand on their own two feet.

My initial meeting with the gentleman did not disappoint. He was friendly, eloquent and witty with a great sense of humour. But always you were aware of the razor-sharp mind that could quote a mortgage payment or a return on investment.

Over the years, I had the pleasure of having lunch with Joe from time to time. To me, these were important events, like getting a tutorial about the most important issues I could face. I told one of my colleagues it was like getting an MBA on life, what to think about, what to do. At times, Joe would call me out, put me on the spot. He spoke about giving back to the community, but not just in the normal, routine ways. He talked about my heritage, how the Japanese community in Vancouver was once a vibrant, wonderful community that made a solid contribution to the fabric of the city. After the war, the community was quiet, more withdrawn, and this saddened him. He told me it was my duty as a senior member of the business community to do what I could to bring that vibrancy back.

Shortly thereafter I joined the Nikkei Society, which promotes cultural awareness of the Japanese community.

Joe told me I would have several careers in my lifetime, some of which might involve business, some of which might involve philanthropy. "Giving," he said, "is only impactful when it hurts a bit." At one luncheon several years ago, he said to me, "We really don't have business luncheons, do we?" and I had to agree. Although we did many deals between our companies, these times were different, special. At one of the last luncheons I can recall, Joe said to me he would give me a fortune to trade places with me. When I asked him why, he said I had something he didn't have – I had time on my side. Another fortune can always be made, but you have to have time to do it and enjoy it.

Joe also taught me a valuable lesson in negotiating deals. He said, "A deal has to be good for both parties. If someone feels like you got the better of him, he will likely never do business with you again. You gain an enemy, not a friend. If you both leave a little on the table, you are both happy, and you will likely do more business in future." This philosophy has been the underlying factor in my company landing some major deals over the years.

Joe Segal is a remarkable man who has had a tremendous influence on the way I think and hopefully the way I act. Thanks, Joe, for being that one in a million people who walks the talk, who has risen above the crowd.

CHAPTER 37

SUKI SEKHON

CEO, CRS Group Companies

In March of 1998 I travelled to India with Joe and Rose Segal and a few friends to attend a wedding in New Delhi. I was planning to attend the wedding and then afterwards meet my mother in Ludhiana to visit our remaining relatives in India whom I had never met before to mourn the recent passing of my father. I had known Joe for years prior to the trip, but I really got to know the "real Joe" as we travelled together over the next few weeks.

During the trip Joe amazed me with his energy, enthusiasm and most of all, his interest in the Indian culture. We travelled for days by bus and visited many of the historical sites in New Delhi, Agra and Jaipur. Upon our return to New Delhi we attended many wedding functions. An Indian wedding is usually a five-day event, and during one of those events Joe could feel that I was very disturbed by my father's death and could see that I could use some fatherly advice. He encouraged me to stand by my family and to pursue my goals now, as I was still young (age 33). He said, "You can still make mistakes and recover from them at your age, but given your business acumen you will be successful." With Joe's encouragement and feeling that I needed a change, I returned from my trip and decided to set up my own company to pursue my lifelong dream of controlling my own destiny. Even though I had lost my father, I gained a person who mentored me and has made a real difference in my life.

Over the past few years Joe has continued to be a mentor and we have established an even closer bond through business ventures, charity work and other community-related activities. I have been blessed to spend time with the man we all call "JS" and I am proud to be his friend.

CHAPTER 38

GRAHAM MACLACHLAN

Regional President, RBC Royal Bank

I have had the pleasure of having had "Lunch With Joe" on several occasions at the Four Seasons. I always looked forward to these lunches for the opportunity to listen to the life lessons from an icon in the Vancouver business community, which Joe is very willing to share. Webster's dictionary defines wisdom as "the quality of being wise, power of judging rightly and following the soundest course of action, based on knowledge, experience, understanding; good judgment." To me this is a very accurate description of Joe Segal; however, he is also much more than this. He has accumulated this wisdom over a long lifetime of experiences and incredible achievements and is generous with sharing not only his money but his insights. He dispenses them with clarity and a wonderful sense of humour on many subjects, whether it be business, family, relationships or philanthropy, just to name a few. I have attended many events and witnessed Joe giving back to the community through countless donations to many wonderful causes. His advice that we should each give what we can afford, regardless of the amount, because we can, has stuck with me. Joe has a wonderful ability to see situations, even complex ones, for what they are; to get to the essence of a problem or challenge and communicate a commonsense practical solution that leaves the recipient thinking: that makes so much sense and is so clear and obvious, why didn't I think of that? That is his gift of insight and intelligence. A dedicated family man, successful in business, generous, community minded, loyal and operating off a strong foundation of values, he has been a role model to me, and those of us who have been fortunate to share some time with him, come away from the experience a little wiser and a bit more motivated to make a difference.

CHAPTER 39

HONOURABLE CHRISTY CLARK

Premier, Province of British Columbia

I was first elected to the legislature in 1996, thinking I had a great start in doing what I wanted to do with my life – politics. But in 2005, everything changed. I was blessed with having my son, and decided to leave public life, so that I could spend more time with him.

But a decision to leave something doesn't necessarily lead directly to what comes next – and it was always going to be difficult to find something as compelling as provincial politics. So, I actively sought out good advice on what I should do next.

One person whose advice we always valued is Peter Legge. He took one second to think about it and told me I needed to see Joe. A coffee turned into another coffee, which led to another, which led eventually to a very memorable, and for me, important lunch.

As we discussed my future, Joe looked me hard in the eyes, and stabbed his finger in the air between us. What he said next stuck with me ever since:

"My only advice is this – do what you want. Discover your purpose. And once you do, work at it as hard as you've ever worked at anything."

He could have said, "I think you should do" something or

other, but instead he gave me a piece of advice that's shaped my life ever since.

Fierce passion, vigour and a sense of purpose illuminate and define Joe Segal. Joe leads by example.

It was the best advice I ever got.

CHAPTER 40

HAMID ESHGHI

President, Djavad Mowafaghian Foundation

The first time I heard the Segal name was 26 years after my father-in-law, Abraham Tahsili, had the occasion to meet Joe and Rosalie Segal at their home. He explained to me that when he met them, Rosalie was knitting items to donate to charity. This surprised Abraham and he asked her why she did not simply donate purchased items. She explained that she preferred to make them herself, as it was important for her to be personally involved in her charitable activities and it made her happy to know that these items would carry her love to their recipients. Rosalie Segal, I surmise, is not only Joe Segal's beautiful wife, but also his inspiration when it comes to philanthropy.

My uncle, Djavad Mowafaghian, formed our family foundation 10 years ago and since then, we have had the opportunity to get to know Joe Segal on a more personal level. He has become a very important role model for our Foundation and has provided valuable advice on how we can most effectively help society.

Joe and Rosalie Segal are compassionate philanthropists who have donated countless hours and dollars to benefit society. Their generosity serves as a perfect example of community work and encourages others to follow their lead. Joe and Rosalie Segal are also remarkable parents, who have passed down their tradition of community service and giving to their children and grandchildren. Their children are leaders in many community and charitable initiatives in Vancouver. Their son Lorne, whom I know personally, works tirelessly for charitable organizations and is a master at inspiring others to join in important philanthropic endeavours. The Segal grandchildren are now following in the footsteps of the generations before them. I have attended several events in Vancouver that the Segal grandchildren have either hosted or spoken at. The maturity and sense of purpose that I witnessed demonstrates that the Segal family's commitment to community has been handed down to this youngest generation.

Not long ago, my uncle Djavad Mowafaghian and I spoke to Joe Segal at an event in Vancouver, and he told us that he recently prayed and asked God to let him live to 100 years of ago so he could continue his good work. My uncle and I, along with thousands of others, pray to God that Joe Segal lives to 100 years and far beyond.

CHAPTER 41

TERRY HUI

President & CEO, Concord Pacific Developments Inc.

In the late '80s, I relocated from California to Vancouver. We were in the early stages of rezoning the former Expo Lands known now as Concord Pacific Place. While working on this master plan, we were also looking at a piece of land adjacent to our site to build a couple of towers.

Everyone knew that if there was a transaction involving a good piece of real estate in Vancouver, Joe Segal's name was more than likely attached to it. This piece of land we were looking at was no exception.

I negotiated with Joe on the price for the property and we made a deal with a very short closing. Because of the short closing, we also agreed that the purchase price could be adjusted after closing if a survey revealed the land to be smaller than what was represented to us.

The deal closed uneventfully. A few weeks after the closing, our lawyer reported that a survey was conducted revealing the parcel of land to be slightly larger than the figures provided to us initially. It was a bit unclear on whether an adjustment was applicable in this situation.

I contacted Joe and told him that we had a bit of an issue.

The land size is incorrect; we actually owe you a small cheque. Joe laughed about it and responded by saying, "Well, this is a nice surprise, please send the cheque to the Children's Hospital Foundation instead." We both agreed it was an elegant way to resolve the situation. Upon our donation, B.C. Children's Hospital offered to put our name on newly purchased x-ray equipment. We kindly turned down the offer.

This was among our first donations to local causes in Vancouver. I have to credit Joe for introducing us to local community involvement. Joe's roundabout introduction opened the door to the long relationship that we continue to have to this day with the B.C. Children's Hospital Foundation.

This was our first deal. On an annual basis, over the following two decades, I have done many more transactions with Joe, and with his eldest son, Lorne. One would expect these to be real estate deals. In fact, all the following "transactions" have had to do with charitable and community causes. Since B.C. Children's Hospital, Joe and Lorne have introduced us to other charities, including the Courage to Come Back Awards, We Day and others. I'm sure that others have received similar calls from Joe and Lorne that have more often than not ended in similar fashion.

CHAPTER 42

LINDSAY GORDON

Past President & CEO, HSBC Bank of Canada

"We make a living by what we get, but we make a life by what we give." For me, Churchill's words epitomize Joe and, for that matter, the entire Segal family. I can think of no other living person in Vancouver who has used their good fortune to help the community more than Joe. His business acumen is legendary and he is a trader without equal. I have known Joe for over 20 years, mostly in my capacity at HSBC Bank Canada – in the many meetings and lunches with Joe, I have always appreciated his direct and forthright manner. In fact, there were occasions when I was quite convinced that Joe thought he should be running the bank! I sometimes felt that I should be paying Joe to have him bank with us! However, most conversations ended with Joe speaking warmly about the staff he dealt with and how important they were to the bank's success. Joe is someone who appreciates the importance of everyone's contribution to success and I think this stems from his profound belief in the importance of family. As for the community activities he has supported over the years with time and money, the Segal family is without equal. Joe's energy and enthusiasm are legendary and I can only hope that in the years to come, I have half of what keeps Joe ticking. He is a great family man, business leader, community leader, philanthropist, and a role model for me and so many others. British Columbia owes Joe and the entire Segal family a huge debt of gratitude.

CHAPTER 43

ANDREW ROSENBLATT

Rabbi, Congregation Schara Tzedeck

I was not privileged to view the other entries of this book when writing my own entry. I have to imagine many of them reference business acumen or the magnitude of the generosity of Joseph and Rosalie Segal, such as large gifts to Vancouver General Hospital, Simon Fraser University, VanDusen Gardens, Schara Tzedeck Synagogue, to name a small few.

I have been privileged to see Joe and Rosalie's generosity from a different perspective. One which has deep roots in Jewish tradition. The code of Jewish law famously delineates that one must tithe, give a minimum of 10 per cent of one's earnings to charity. However, it is less well known that when giving to the poor, one should act in the best interest of the needy individual's self-esteem. One must be patient, of pleasant disposition and where possible, give anonymously.

Joe Segal follows this tradition intuitively. I came to know this because there was an individual, who for the sake of anonymity, we will call Glenn. Glenn would often visit to request funds from the Schara Tzedeck Rabbi's discretionary fund. Glenn had once been wealthy but lost much of his money on high-risk investments and horse racing. He had not entirely given up the life of a gambler, and had certainly not given up fabricating unlikely stories. There is little surprise that he was often in need of funds. Joe Segal not only honoured Glenn's request for charity, he would also spend hours with Glenn listening to his troubles, stories and woes. When I think about what an hour of Joe Segal's time is worth, I find myself particularly inspired by the respectful way in which he treated this destitute individual. Furthermore, I know that Glenn was not one single individual; there have been many similar individuals in this manner, and Joe has not locked his door to these individuals. In fact, he personally makes gifts to the Synagogue to make sure that the charity fund has sufficient means to care for similar cases.

These are not the kind of charitable gifts that get your name printed in a program, or affixed to the facade of a building; they are, however, the most sensitive and inspired acts of charity. They are the kind of charity that the Torah prizes most highly for they are an investment in personal dignity as much as, if not more than, in economic relief.

CHAPTER 44

RON DOMOUCHELLE

Past President & CEO, VGH & UBC Hospital Foundation

"There but for the grace of God go I."

As I have had the unique privilege of getting to know Joe over the past 20 years, I've come to understand why this phrase is so apropos to him.

Joe, the extremely successful, legendary businessman and philanthropist, was also Joe, the common man, who never forgot his roots, and his journey.

One day, 15 years ago, I was meeting with Joe in his office. As I was arriving, someone was just leaving. Joe explained how he didn't really know the person well, having just met him a few weeks ago, but he was struck by his hard luck story, and had given him some money. The man had just come by to thank Joe again for helping him out. Joe then showed me a large ledger he kept, a record of his charitable assistance disbursements to people and causes. For the current year, pages and pages. Hundreds of entries. All sizes and amounts. Joe helping so many people.

For such an accomplished entrepreneur and businessman, a skilled negotiator, Joe has the heart of a loving puppy, a special regard for the everyday man, for people in need, people having a rough time.

Fast forward to fall 2010. After many conversations over many months, Joe and Rosalie made a decision to commit the lead donation of $12 million for a new mental health pavilion at VGH, one that will eventually help people from all walks of life who are struggling with one form or another of mental illness. Part of Joe's rationale for his decision was — "I didn't want to support the obvious. I want to help where it's most needed. Mental illness is kind of out of sight, out of mind, and there's a tendency to sweep it under the carpet. But you walk the face of the earth and say, 'There but for the grace of God go I.' "

I, along with Jim O'Hara, my friend and colleague from VGH & UBC Hospital Foundation, have met with Joe many times over the years, and we would usually come away with a story or two or three. It was always a rich and rewarding part of our Joe Segal relationship, one that both of us will always cherish. We would often leave with the feeling that Joe had taken special pleasure in goodheartedly toying with us, imparting a lesson or two. We were the young pups learning from the top dog.

Thanks, Joe.

CHAPTER 45

DAVID POOLE

Senior Vice-President, BC & Yukon Region, Scotiabank

As a transplanted person from Ontario I did not have the benefit of knowing the background of Joe Segal until I arrived in Vancouver in 2006. I believe I was only here two days before I met Joe at the Courage to Come Back Awards where he generously made a leadership gift that encouraged several other people to donate as well. Over the past seven years, I have heard Joe speak at several charitable functions where Rosalie and Joe were being honoured for their generosity and philanthropic support. Joe has a very simple concept, which he shares willingly: "If you have more than enough for yourself, why not share the rest with people that need it more?" Another concept is his ability to rationalize why we are attending a fundraising event: If you are suffering with the health ailment we are raising funds for, then you appreciate everyone's efforts. If you aren't, you should be thankful you will feel better if you donate to the cause especially when you have more money than you need.

I have had the privilege of having "Lunch With Joe" on several occasions and firstly I was impressed at his knowledge of my background and of what charities I was involved in. He made me feel very comfortable and made it very clear if I needed something, to just ask. He greatly assisted several charities I was directly involved with, including opening up his home with Rosalie to assist in fundraising. This to me is the ultimate commitment on someone's part to support their community.

I look forward to my next "Lunch With Joe" and congratulate him on the tremendous legacy he has created not only for himself but for the Segal family.

CHAPTER 46

PHILIP TEAL MD

Professor of Neurology, UBC

It is both an honour and a daunting privilege to try to encapsulate in a few hundred words some aspects of the remarkable life to date of Joe Segal.

As I reflect on my interactions with Joe over the past several years, I realize that I have been fortunate to know an extraordinary individual who has led, and continues to lead, an extraordinary life.

Where to begin when there is so much to consider? This question has kept me awake.

Business savvy – check. Joe is a business genius. I will leave Joe's business expertise and financial success to others in a better position to comment. It is an enlightening experience to watch Joe mentally calculate the wisdom of a business deal. Real estate, manufacturing, financial services, retail merchandising – check, check, check and check. Joe seems to know it all.

Philanthropy – check. Joe sets the standard for all around him. No worthy issue is too large or, perhaps more importantly, too small to escape his attention and support. The recent generosity of Joe and Rosalie Segal to support mental health care is only one example of how Joe is a champion of the disadvantaged and underserved.

Leadership – check. Like any gifted leader, Joe leads by example and makes all around him perform better. Integrity – check. Joe has said that he wishes he had gone into politics at some point in his life. I am sure that we all would have benefited from his leadership and integrity had they been applied to provincial or national politics.

It is Joe's humanity, mental toughness, charisma and great humour that are truly distinguishing qualities of his character.

One of my initial encounters with Joe was in the medical context. Often when one is confronted by personal illness the true strength and character of an individual is exposed. When Joe was in hospital under my care, it was clear that he was more concerned with the wellbeing of Rose than with his own condition. Rather that dwelling on himself he was busy planning a major donation to develop a new centre for mental health and planning how he and Rosalie could acknowledge the nurses who cared for him. These are examples of Joe's recognition of the large and small needs of others and his mental toughness under trying times. Fortunately all turned out well.

It was also in the medical context that I realized how significantly Joe and Rosalie had connected on a personal level with Vancouver General Hospital. When I rushed to see him in the ER for a medical issue in my zone, I found there were already four nervous cardiologists wringing their hands at his bedside. As I left to look at his test results, I bumped into a fifth cardiologist on his way to see him. Pretty impressive, particularly as there were no cardiac issues. Their concern was for Joe's wellbeing and they were there to ensure that things were looked after.

Recently, my family was inspired by Joe's wisdom in personal matters and the conduct of successful relationships. During an engagement celebration for Gillian, our oldest daughter, and Adam Segal, Joe's grandson, Joe spoke with his customary eloquence about the qualities necessary for an enduring and successful marriage. I am sure that Joe's advice on the importance of communication will serve them well throughout their lives together. We are grateful for this acquired wisdom that was passed on to them. The durability and success of Joe and Rosalie's marriage bears testimony to the fact that he not only talks the talk but also walks the walk.

Joe always has a twinkle in his eye, a humorous comment or insight, and a personal inquiry to make. He loves a good laugh and to innocently flirt and charm. It is amazing that one individual has so many skills and is so respected in all his affairs both personal and business.

Joe is loved by family, friends and business associates.

On a personal level, the intersection of our lives with Joe and Rosalie Segal and their family has been profoundly rewarding. I am sure there are many thousands who feel the same way.

Joe Segal — truly an extraordinary man.

CHAPTER 47

MICHAEL STEVENSON

President Emeritus, Simon Fraser University

As the newly appointed President of SFU, I was introduced to Joe as soon as we arrived in Vancouver. He was, as always, direct. "So, you're the new guy from Toronto who thinks he can manage our university?"

There was the ever-present twinkle in his eye, but his question was loaded with implication. Rather than taking the bait, I said something banal about a determination to do my best. He may have been disappointed at this lack of courage, because our first meeting ended with a warning: "Well, we'll be watching you. Just don't screw it up."

Many more social encounters followed over the next 18 months, when Joe was always jovial and always had the same question: "Do you realize yet how lucky you are to be living in the best place on earth?" Enthusiastic in the affirmative, I avoided betraying my uneasiness that, while I had not yet screwed up, I had, so far, done little to make my mark at "our" university.

I was surprised, therefore, to get a personal call from Joe inviting me to lunch to discuss an opportunity for SFU. At his table in Chartwell, my anxiety was piqued by reference to his war experience and to learning the lessons of guts and leadership from the great Prime Minister in whose ambience we met. My grasp of Churchilliana was shaky, but I had a recollection that it was he who had rejected an unworthy as someone who "never missed an opportunity to miss an opportunity."

Lunch progressed with proper respect to the great leader's appetites: a giant martini and a considerable portion of a superb Chardonnay. I was not, therefore, prepared for Joe's quick turn to business, let alone for his lightning-quick arithmetic when he flushed out his proposal. Again, he began directly:

"Your predecessors made SFU's downtown campus the intellectual heart of Vancouver. What will you do to build that legacy?"

As I muttered my admiration for past achievements and determination to build on them, he interrupted:

"What would you do if you could get another building, something like the Wosk Centre?"

At last I could say something about every great city having a successful business school at its core; that I would move the graduate programs of SFU Business into a new branded site, filling the space they released at Harbour Centre with new programs responding to the city's interests in urban studies, international affairs and communications. Again, I was interrupted before I could sound convincing.

"All that sounds good," Joe said, "but I need to know whether you have the balls to get something like this done."

My memory of the next hour is blurred but the impact

unforgettable. Joe thought Vancouver's historic Bank of Montreal headquarters might be available. He told me of his long banking history at that location, and without a note gave a lovingly detailed description of the building's architectural plan. He embellished this picture of a great heritage structure with rapid-fire details about its FSR, the likely current market value, the potential value of heritage bonus provisions, and other development industry specifics beyond my comprehension.

"So, if I got you this building, would you be able to manage the costs of a superb renovation, the ongoing costs of the highest standard maintenance, and fundraising for the endowment you say is needed to put SFU Business into world-class competition?"

By this point, I was wishing that I had not been so specific, and hoped that a post-lunch hangover would not force a recantation. But, with some trepidation, I assured him it would all be done, as long as I could rely on his advice and support.

"Okay," he said, "let's talk more later. I'm late. Remember how lucky you are to live in the best city on earth."

We talked much more, of course, in the following months, and Joe was always as insistent that we clarify the strategic vision for the project as he was that we master the development details. As a result of his generous gift, SFU obtained this great jewel in the crown of its Vancouver campus. As a result of his passion for architectural detail and respect for tradition, the jewel was cut and polished to perfection by a great Vancouver architect. As a result of his prestige in the community, we raised the considerable funds required for a truly dramatic renovation, and as he always promised, his gift of the building led subsequently to other contributions to academic excellence. SFU's Segal Graduate School of Business thus stands as the finest home of an urban business school, with academic programs now endowed by the exceptional generosity of Joe's protégé, Ryan Beedie. And a university president was saved from screwing up by the most generous of mentors and friends.

CHAPTER 48

GARY SEGAL

Vice President, Kingswood Capital Corporation

He is "Mr. Segal" to some or simply "Joe" to others. He has been recognized far and wide as a Hall of Fame businessman and entrepreneur, real estate legend, Second World War vet, community leader, mentor, philosopher and philanthropist. To me, he is all that and so much more – he is my father.

Were there one or more seminal events in his younger years that might have played a role in shaping the man and his eventual success? Perhaps dropping out of high school to help support the family after his father Samuel's early death? Maybe the two years of dangerous army service overseas during the Second World War? Was it the severe hay fever? (More on this later.)

Some may wonder what it is like growing up with a father like Joe Segal. My childhood memories are not of going fishing, playing tennis or golfing with my father. While that would have been nice, truth is I do not lament that fact. The moments of quality time my father did manage to set aside for the children meant a lot. At the same time, our devoted mother Rosalie was always there to nurture and take care of us while my father was busy building a solid future for wife, family and community.

The father-son time I may have missed out on growing up has

been more than balanced out by the opportunity to interact with him every day at work over the last 28 years. There are so many things I have learned to admire about my father; it is not about his extraordinary success per se; rather, the amazing combination of qualities and traits that he possesses. To list just a few:

His drive for independence and sense of responsibility that he exhibited at a young age;

His "superhuman" memory and powers of observation;

His generous nature and lifetime commitment to giving back to the community;

His compassion for the underdog;

His innate gift of being able to "read" people, size up a situation and get to the heart of a matter immediately;

His sense of urgency and ability to look forward and put the past behind and;

His unwavering integrity and wisdom.

His life is the ultimate example of one of the fundamental principles he preaches: "You get out of life what you put into it." My father has been rewarded for his success, both monetarily and with a certain respect or influence that comes along with it, but as he would tell anyone in a similar position, what good are those rewards unless you choose to do great things with them? My father does not live for the money or accolades – his satisfaction is from the doing, the building and contributing.

Since my childhood, both my parents have been shining examples of the importance of philanthropy and giving back to the community, both in terms of time and money. In addition to their many well-known acts of largess are the many acts of charity and kindness they quietly extend to a regular stream of people or organizations that may be faced with hard times or that nobody else cares about.

In life and business not every situation has a good solution or ending. The immaculate reputation my father has maintained over his lengthy and prominent business career attests to the fact that he goes out of his way to treat people fairly and does what is right and ethical, not what is most profitable or convenient.

There are so many other remarkable and noteworthy things about my father that have left an impression on me and from which everyone could learn. It amazes me how my father seems to know something about everything, but that is no accident. Though my father never finished high school, he more than made up for it by being a voracious reader of all kinds of publications. Coupled with his extraordinary memory, tireless work effort, uncanny perception and an abundance of common sense, you have what is perceived as genius.

When my father talks, people listen. He is a marvellous raconteur, able to engage people with a story and disarm them with charm. Somehow he gets away with asking people the most personal or delicate of questions that no one else would dare even think to ask. He loves to engage the world in conversation, from the server, doorman or cab driver, to a perfect stranger in an elevator, at a restaurant table or on the street. He is interested in people and perfectly willing to offer them advice they may not even know they could use.

I can tell you that beneath a sometimes-tough exterior is a man of great emotion, caring and compassion. And when all is said and done, nothing means more to him than family, and there is no one he admires and loves more than my mother.

I truly have been blessed to share countless illuminating, insightful and irreplaceable moments with one of the world's great men — moments I will cherish and remember forever. By the way, one of the great perks that comes with my position: front of the line priority status for booking lunch with Joe!

P.S. About that hay fever: Quite recently I discovered that very early in his working career some friends tried to get my father interested in golfing, but with his severe allergies he found the experience unbearable and had to abandon the thought. While I may have lost a father to golf with — who knows — perhaps a potential distraction from Joe's destiny with greatness was nipped in the bud?

CHAPTER 49

HONOURABLE WALLACE T. OPPAL Q.C.

Broughton Law Corporation

The greatness of any city is measured by the greatness of its citizens. Vancouver is said to be a great city. No one person has contributed to its greatness more than Joe Segal.

Joe Segal is the well-known and highly recognized founder of Kingswood Capital Corporation. Kingswood Capital is a major developer of real estate holdings in Vancouver, in Western Canada and Washington State. As well, he has played an integral role in the corporate life of British Columbia for over 40 years.

It is important to note, however, that this remarkable self-made man had humble beginnings. After having served Canada overseas in the Second World War, he came to Vancouver in 1946 and began a war-surplus business. Thereafter he established Fields Stores Ltd. and later purchased some 240 franchise stores of Marshall-Wells Wholesale Hardware. Mr. Segal has been said by many to be a true legend among entrepreneurs in Western Canada but more than that he has made a tremendous contribution to public life. He was the Chancellor of Simon Fraser University after being on its board for over 12 years. He helped establish the university's downtown campus. In 2005, his family contributed to the establishment of the Simon Fraser University Segal Graduate School of Business in downtown Vancouver.

Beyond the obvious successes he has achieved in business, Mr. Segal is a person of compassion and generosity and has shown that he genuinely cares for others. He has been a contributor to virtually every charity in this province and as recognition for his many years of public service he has been awarded both the Order of British Columbia and the Order of Canada, one of the few people in this province who has been recognized in such a way.

From a personal perspective, I must comment on Mr. Segal's donation of $12 million for the establishment of a new mental health facility at Vancouver General Hospital. There is a clear need for such a facility. I have been in the criminal justice system for over 40 years as a lawyer, a Crown Counsel, a judge, Attorney General and a Commissioner of Inquiries. I have seen firsthand the effects of mental illness as they are played out in the justice system. The cause and effects of mental illness are sorely neglected in our society. Many, many crimes are committed by persons who are suffering from mental disorders or mental incapacity. Acts of violence that often have devastating consequences are often the result of mental illness. By addressing the causes and cures of mental disorders, we can truly address some of the root causes of crime. The Segal family must be commended for its much-needed support for mental illness.

I see Mr. Segal frequently. He generates a genuine warmth of personality. He is truly a caring person. We in British Columbia are indeed fortunate to have him amongst us.

CHAPTER 50

DR. ELI KONORTI P.Eng.

Advantage Management Solutions

"Doctor, how are you?"

"I'm fine, JS, thanks."

"What's up?"

"Well, JS, we had a good day. Our sales were above average, we shipped a lot, the productivity and quality were great, and cash flow was positive."

This was my daily 6 p.m. telephone conversion with Joe Segal (or JS, as I call him) that continued for the entire nine years we were business partners.

To the average person or businessman, this might seem odd or even boring; the same questions, every day. Nevertheless, to the pragmatic businessman, these questions are paramount. Simply put, JS focused on the three to five pieces of information that tell you exactly how a business is doing. JS knew this long before business executives started talking about such things as dashboards or scorecards. I call this innate wisdom.

In the years since, I have frequently used JS's pearls of wisdom in my own life as well as to help my clients better manage their businesses. My favourite is "You can't ride two horses with one ass," as it invariably delivers a clear message that is easily understood.

Another favourite is "Stay with the best and get rid of the rest," which is quite simply the answer to many business problems. It is no wonder that people think of JS not only as a generous and highly successful businessman, but one who is wise "beyond his years."

CHAPTER 51

SAUL KAHN

Son of Leon Kahn, O.B.M., Co-founder of Laurelton Investment Ltd.

I've known Joe Segal since I was a young boy (I still call him "Mr. Segal" despite being 52) thanks to his lengthy business relationship and friendship with my late father, Leon Kahn (of blessed memory).

My father emigrated from Europe to Canada on September 9, 1948. With no family, no money, no English, not even a high school diploma (like Mr. Segal, his education had been cut short in Grade 10 due to the war), the odds appeared to be stacked against him. However, Canada turned out to truly be the "land of opportunity" for my father. After 13 years of success with Block Bros. Industries, in 1968 my father embarked on what would become a very fruitful 35-year business relationship with Mr. Segal.

The two men were cut from much the same cloth, assertive, hard-working, tenacious and strong-willed, qualities that caused them to butt heads from time to time; however, they also shared a mutual respect and deep admiration for one another, which explains why their relationship not only survived but thrived until my father's sudden and untimely passing in June of 2003.

Looking back on his life, Abraham Joshua Heschel, one of the leading Jewish philosophers of the 20th century, remarked,

"When I was young I admired clever people. Now that I'm old I admire kind people," the implication being that these two qualities don't normally go together. My father was an exception to this generalization and I know he recognized the same in his friend and business partner Joe Segal.

Indeed, in contemplation of his death, my father recorded a number of deeply personal thoughts for my mother, siblings and me to always bear in mind, including:

"You can consult with Joe Segal; he's got a good heart and will give you good advice."

Those words are as true today as they were when my father wrote them more than a decade ago. I've heeded my father's advice on numerous occasions and on each one Mr. Segal has demonstrated great kindness, patience and magnanimity while offering his many years of wisdom and experience. For this and so much more, my family and I are eternally grateful.

CHAPTER 52

RUDY NORTH

CEO, North Growth Management

Joe was already an iconic business figure when I started my career as a stock analyst. One of my first assignments was to look into Fields stores. Straight out of university, I was still nervous about management interviews. Many Canadian top executives were uncommunicative especially back then with young analysts like myself.

Joe was different.

He was quick to say, "Come down to the main store and I'll tell you how we do things." That is the only company visit I still remember from those days. Joe was enthusiastically running a hands-on innovative business ahead of its time in inventory systems, buying philosophy and stores that gave customers what they wanted at great prices.

Joe was instantly a person I wished I had a chance to know personally. That chance came years later when Joe set out to teach Vancouver it was okay to give! That was in the early '80s when the United Way told me that they had only received three donations of $10,000 or more that year. About the same time they contacted Joe to thank him profusely for his donation and ask if he would do the same the following year.

My understanding is that Joe scolded them for such a lame approach, and said something to the effect of, "You should be asking me if I could give more next year! Doubling my donation would be better!"

There was a lot of wealth in Vancouver even back then. Joe felt that Vancouver could do better and offered to show the United Way how to go about it. He contacted many friends and acquaintances and challenged them to give $5,000 or more and hosted annual dinners for all those who did so.

These events were characteristic Joe – upbeat, friendly and inspirational. In subsequent years, his philanthropic "club membership" grew. Soon there were not just three donations of $10,000 or more, there were tens and then hundreds of such donations.

A whole new attitude towards charitable giving evolved in Vancouver and, of course, Joe was at the forefront of it all.

CHAPTER 53

BOB RENNIE

Principal, Rennie Marketing Systems

Today:

I sit at my table in the Four Seasons Yew restaurant, across from Joe at his table, too many times a week. And no matter who is joining me for lunch, Joe makes the time to make them feel good about who they are and what they do. As I leave the restaurant, more often than not, Joe will pull me over to his table and engage his lunch guests (I cannot believe the range of company this man keeps) and myself, with gracious, gracious, gracious and generous words, that make us all feel very special and *Joe does not even realize!*

1990:

Dan Ulinder, my business partner at the time, would often tell me (at the time I was a house salesman in Burnaby) about his interactions with the great Joe Segal.

"Dan . . . find one thing and do it better than anybody else," Dan would recite his conversations with Joe Segal, this, at a time when Dan was figuring life out. I listened to the advice that Joe Segal gave to my friend Dan. *Joe does not even realize!*

1992:

Dan Ulinder and I went to the Four Seasons Hotel for lunch

at Chartwell, and sitting at a table was Joe Segal, this man who doesn't realize how he has influenced my life through his talks with Dan. Joe Segal was about to influence my life again, and until reading this, I'm quite certain he doesn't even realize how. Joe Segal was not just at a table, not just any table, but his table. This fascinated me and still does to this day. To have my own table became a lifetime goal. To simply observe Joe Segal is enough, to engage is an honour.

Do we ever really know, when we are influenced by another? *Joe does not even realize, and neither did I until I took a moment to reflect on my journeys with Joe!*

CHAPTER 54

MORAY B. KEITH

President, Dueck Autogroup

Recently I was on a panel at the Annual Jewish Community Centre Breakfast. The panel was made up of sports celebrities Charmaine Crooks and Bob Lenarduzzi and sports commentator Jim Robson. I suppose I was there to represent the business side of sports. It was an honour to be on the same panel.

At one point, the moderator asked each of us to name a person who has been influential in our lives, someone who has mentored or motivated us or is someone we'd like to emulate. As the other panellists identified and described their key person, I was surprised at how easy it was for me to pick my role model – Joe Segal.

Now don't misunderstand, I wasn't picking Joe as my sports hero, or as a racing great, nor did I assume this was a category for my biggest supporter. I am taller than Joe, I want to be a better athlete, maybe a better golfer, but those weren't the qualities or reasons I consider Joe Segal to be special. His qualities that inspire me are: his devotion to family and friends, his philanthropy and his love for business.

The patriarch in the Segal family ensures the family is wonderfully close. I have admired that since I met Joe in the '80s. The love, the unity and the support for one another is very special in a world where there are so many diversions.

There will be many people in this book who speak with more knowledge of Joe's philanthropy. However, I have seen firsthand his remarkable acts of giving, many of which have been without recognition. Helping individuals through tough periods or prompting someone to do better, taking the time to care, that's Joe.

Do you ever notice how with really great people they always focus on you in a conversation? They don't look past you to see who is next through the door. They are genuinely interested in you! Joe is one of those people. Money helps immensely, in some circumstances, but so does taking the time to listen and provide thoughtful guidance. That's very special. I remember Joe's comments to me when we were talking about giving. "Giving isn't giving, until it hurts," he said.

Lastly, and this is perhaps a key factor for me in identifying Joe as my inspiration for the future, is his love for business.

Where many people use business as a means to an end, Joe enjoys the day-to-day activity. Creating deals, doing deals — I honestly think that is what has kept him so sharp and relevant. I want to be in my 80s, going to my office (on my schedule) dreaming of what could be, meeting with my kids and close friends . . . and of course, schooling the odd upstart. Enjoying the odd cigar and reminiscing on my learnings from a life well lived.

There's one quick story I'd like to share before I go. In the early '80s, I needed to acquire property and move our Dueck on Marine auto dealership. An icon in Vancouver since 1926, it was important to find an ideal location. Joe owned property just down the street and I had already met Joe socially at a number of functions, so I got in touch with him.

Joe's belief in the value of the property, and my limited finances as we built equity in our business, restricted the opportunity for a deal at the time. Shortly after our meeting, SFU asked me to chair their yearly fundraising campaign. Joe was the Chancellor at SFU.

Through the efforts of many talented people, we raised a record amount that year. At the annual celebration luncheon, Joe quietly moved to my side and suggested I enlist for another year. I was proud to be on his team and did so willingly.

Another year passed and again, thanks to some wonderful hardworking folks who made me look good, we had another record year.

Again at the celebratory luncheon, Joe quietly moved to my side, but this time his comment was one that would change my life: "I think it's time you owned your land and buildings," he said.

"I really want to," I told him.

To which Joe replied, "See you Monday, kid."

On Monday, Joe and I (with no one else present) made a deal that would change my life. He listened, he never forgot, he understood my challenges and did what he called a fair deal.

I learned from Joe that deals should be good for both parties: it was a good deal for Joe and a good deal for me!

It is the wise philosophy of a man who has helped so many — I would like to be like Joe!

CHAPTER 55

PETER Y. ENG N.A., MBA, LL.D.

Chairman, Allied Holdings Ltd.

I have known Joe for easily 30 years. I do not get to see him very often, but whenever I do, I cannot help noticing how youthful-looking he always stays. Just two weeks ago, we were together at a dinner party. I remember on our way home I remarked to my wife Julia that Joe had hardly aged since the time when we first knew him, and, without the slightest hesitation, she agreed. It is not just the way he looks; he somehow radiates a certain youthfulness of spirit which can be infectious.

I remember Peter Newman in his book *Titans* describing Joe as "the most visible titan in town." It is common knowledge within Joe's circle that he would appear for lunch at a designated table in the Four Seasons almost every weekday while he is in town. That seems to tell me two things about him. First is the regularity and discipline in his daily routine. Secondly, he is forever interested in people and in the world around him. Are these some of the things that have kept him young? In any case, it is clear that life has treated Joe very kindly; conversely, I suspect that he must have mastered the right approach to life.

Joe's extraordinary history of philanthropy is a matter of public record. But the monetary figures people hear about, generous as they are, do not tell the whole story.

Back in the late 1990s, I had the privilege of working with Joe on the project for the establishment of a much-needed conference centre for the downtown campus of Simon Fraser University, ultimately to be named the Morris J. Wosk Centre for Dialogue. Joe, the Chancellor of the University, was the chairman of the ad hoc Council for the SFU International Conference Centre on which I served as a member. The project had a succession of hurdles, but I was able to watch at firsthand how Joe, together with Jack Blaney, vice president and later president of the university, quietly and without fanfare, tackled those hurdles one by one, working painstakingly for four years until the facility not only became a reality but was developed to standards of sophistication that were higher than we had originally planned. Joe is every inch a man of action. He is the kind of philanthropist who is generous not only in sharing his wealth but also in devoting his time and whole-hearted attention to the causes he has pledged to support.

Joe Segal is a true son of Canada. In him (and of course in his "other half" Rosalie) are embodied the finest qualities in the Canadian ideal of personal success and wellbeing achieved on the basis of humanity and concern for the interests of others.

CHAPTER 56

IAN GILLESPIE

President, Westbank

Joe has taken on the role of community leader with a natural ease. He was born with the instincts to succeed, but what is interesting to me is his adoption of the role of mentor to an entire generation of entrepreneurs. Being an entrepreneur can be lonely, especially if you did not come from a family with any history in business.

About 10 years ago, Joe, Milan Ilich and I were trying to buy a property in Burnaby, and I drove to Joe's house on Belmont to have him sign the offer to purchase. To a boy from Port Coquitlam, this is one grand house, and Joe is a proud man. The tour of the house started at the front door with the water jet, anti-raccoon device, the story behind the chandelier in the foyer, the pool, the art... eventually we made it up to Joe and Rosalie's bedroom, and I was sitting on the side of Joe's bed while he recounted how he built his business from nothing into one of Canada's strongest private businesses. He ended the conversation with – "Ian, I have one piece of advice for you: no one ever went poor making a little bit of money." It was one of those moments that I will never forget.

Since that bedside mentoring, I have had the pleasure of being Joe's guest at his lunch table on several occasions. These lunch dates are special, not only because Joe is very entertaining, but because of the thought he puts into these lunches beforehand. He treats them as a very valuable use of time. He knows more about my projects than many of my own team; he even knows about the projects that are still just in their infancy, and he knows with remarkable accuracy the general state of our balance sheet. This knowledge allows him to relate the theme of his lunch to what is happening in real time in our business. I come back to the office feeling like I was just given a rare gift, the gift of wisdom, transferred from one generation to the next, just as it has been done for millennia.

One of the many themes Joe has consistently been discussing for several years is how to give generously, and as our little business matures, I hope he will be proud of how we have learned from his example.

Joe epitomizes for me the maxim that we stand on the shoulders of the previous generation.

CHAPTER 57

ROBERT H. LEE C.M., O.B.C., LL.D.

Director & Chairman, The Prospero Group

I've always been a big admirer of Joe's. And it's not just because he is one of the most successful businessmen I know. He is a great man – a devoted family man, a strong supporter of our community, a man of integrity and a great business partner.

In the early part of 2000, I was invited to start a TV station in Vancouver – specifically a multicultural station, which hosted about 30 different languages.

I called up Joe and asked him if he would consider being one of the partners for the station that would be called 'Multi-vision Television' (Channel M). Neither of us had any experience working in television, but about 10 minutes into the phone conversation, Joe enthusiastically said, "Yes, I'm in. This could be fun."

We were neophytes of the media business, but because all five partners were successful businessmen and we had chosen an impressive group of advisors, we beat out Rogers. To our surprise, the CRTC granted us a license, and we embarked on this new venture.

I believe the station operated quite well compared to other TV stations largely due to the fact that we had very good advisors, a strong management team and an excellent relationship with the bank that helped carry us over the difficult periods. Television is a tough business, and even though we were losing money, we still had a lot of fun.

In the end we learned that in television, you only make money when you sell. Not knowing this, we ended up losing five million a year during the time we owned it.

Five years later, with still just the one TV station (which wasn't proving to be very profitable), we complained to the CRTC that we needed two or three more stations. As it happened, Alberta was going to award two new licenses in Edmonton and one in Calgary. We tendered on all of them and, although I think we gave the best presentations, we lost to Rogers.

Rogers, at the time, owned all the multicultural stations across Canada except for Vancouver, so they approached the partnership to purchase Channel M. Three weeks later, we sold it to Rogers. We were very fortunate to recover our losses and even made a profit. But, as Joe reminded me, "Most importantly, we had fun."

I consider Joe to be one of my mentors. He has always been a very good partner and a very good friend.

CHAPTER 58

MARK HANNAH

Principal, Avison Young Commercial Real Estate

In 2010, I met with Mr. Segal to prepare for a two-part Legend Interview series for an upcoming NAIOP Breakfast. My role as the interviewer was to pose questions on his distinguished business career.

I was fascinated by the story of how his career began. At the tender age of 20, after serving Canada in the Second World War, he launched his first business venture by purchasing excess military medical supplies and equipment for pennies on the dollar and then reselling for quarters on the dollar. This included medical supplies to doctors, paint to farmers, and jeeps and trucks to forestry industry, just to name a few examples.

I was speechless. Who would have the vision and the business savvy to undertake and successfully complete this venture? This first business venture no doubt paved the way for an incredible career in the retail industry followed by an even more impressive track record in commercial real estate. Mr. Segal constantly emphasizes that the key to acquiring real estate is the initial acquisition cost.

Most everyone who knows Mr. Segal would agree that he is likely one of the very few people in business where "his word is his bond," no listing agreement or written document is required.

He has a voracious appetite for information on the market and always ends every telephone conversation with, "What else is happening?" He is constantly gathering and processing information that no doubt has contributed to his success.

The countless meetings I have had sitting on the couch in his office (which he finally reupholstered!) discussing different real estate deals and/or opportunities have been invaluable to me.

During those many meetings in his office and lunches at the Four Seasons (where he would never let anyone pay!) I learned some very valuable lessons that I am grateful for and will pass along to my family and friends.

Lessons learned include: the significance of involving yourself in charity and donating what you can afford to give; the strategy of creating value and generating income in real estate holdings; the value of patience especially when acquiring and/or holding real estate; the importance of integrity, honour and respect.

Mr. Segal often says. "You can't ride two horses with one ass." He is right, but he is probably the only one who could, and it would never bother anyone!

He has set a very high standard that will be difficult for anyone to emulate. I feel very fortunate to have met and learned from the best. The main highlight in my commercial real estate career has not been a specific property sold or deal completed. It is without hesitation that I got to work with and for Mr. Joseph Segal.

Thank you, Mr. Segal, for the lessons learned.

CHAPTER 59

SHIRLEY BROADFOOT

Chair, Coast Mental Health Foundation

I first met Joe after the Courage to Come Back Awards gala in 2000. Coast Mental Health was just getting the awards off the ground at the time. Although its primary focus is to recognize courageous people who have faced and overcome incredible odds, the awards also served as a sort of "coming out party" for our organization. At the time very few people knew much about mental health and fewer people had heard of Coast. Following the event, Joe told me how much he had enjoyed the evening, but he let me know (in that wonderful charming way he has with a twinkle in his eye) that we needed to learn a thing or two about raising money. And did we ever! We are still learning from Joe and Rosalie's generosity and community spirit. As a longtime supporter of mental health services, I am so grateful to them for shining a light on a cause that so many people shy away from.

Luckily for Coast, Joe and Rosalie's son Lorne agreed to chair the Courage to Come Back Awards and take us under his wing.

Over the years Joe and I have had many brief conversations, but recently I had the honour of being invited to have lunch with him one on one and I enjoyed every minute.

Not only is he a gracious host and an engaging storyteller, but he has a knack for bringing the conversation around to things you really care about and he is intent on finding out why they matter so much to you. The conversation led to the connection between happiness, resilience and a positive outlook, and how our physical health is really dependent upon our mental health and sense of wellbeing.

I believe the root of Joe's greatness is his generosity of spirit and his humanity. He sees the things we all have in common, no matter what path our lives have taken and he starts there.

We are all so lucky Joe met Rosalie, "the girl of his dreams," here in Vancouver and decided to make this wonderful city his home.

CHAPTER 60

DON HARRISON

Senior Vice President, Asset Management, GWL Realty Advisors Inc.

Joe is intuitive by nature and has a natural curiosity about people. I met Joe briefly at a real estate function very shortly after moving to Vancouver in 2004. He called me a couple of days later inquiring about how our organization hedged U.S. currency exposure. After explaining that we were not actively investing in U.S. real estate and therefore currency hedging was not relevant, his response was "never mind, we should have lunch." Through his eyes during our first lunch, I learned more about the history of real estate in Vancouver, and retailing in Canada, than I could have imagined possible in two hours. More importantly, it was the beginning of a personal relationship where wittingly or unwittingly, Joe has become a much-valued mentor in my life. My initial impressions remain undiminished – first and foremost Joe is an inquisitive, big-picture guy. In sports vernacular, he doesn't focus on where the puck is, he focuses on where the puck is going to be. He has the wisdom, patience and financial capacity to be an astute and nimble buyer and seller when warranted by market conditions. The downside is that it makes you wonder whether you want to be on either end of these transactions, which we have laughed about on more than one occasion!

Part of Joe's success is that he is not all about business – priorities that always come up in conversations are family, health, commitment to community and career (yours, not his). Sometimes in life you have the privilege to meet someone who simply inspires you to be better. That's just what Joe does.

CHAPTER 61

GRACE M. McCARTHY O.C., O.B.C., LL.D, D.Tech., FRAIC (Hon)

Chairman of the Board, C.H.I.L.D. Foundation

I well remember the lunch with Joe at the Vancouver Four Seasons Hotel. It was 1995 when we met at that special table always reserved for Joe Segal.

I explained my mission, which was to launch a research centre at B.C. Children's Hospital. It would be the first of its kind in British Columbia and would focus on Crohn's disease, ulcerative colitis and liver disorders (biliary atresia).

There was no research being done in British Columbia on these health issues at that time. Once diagnosed (and quite often misdiagnosed) the children affected would live the rest of their lives without a normal childhood. The inflammatory bowel disease (IBD) would continue into adulthood, leading to constant pain and inability to participate in school or take a job, all the while suffering embarrassment among peers and undergoing treatment resulting in a regimen of many pills each day and several stays in hospital to remove the colon or to undergo a colostomy or bowel bypass.

In those days, these children's disorders were unknown to most in the medical world and most of the public, even parents with children so afflicted, found it difficult to talk about such devastating illnesses. As one of the doctors at B.C. Children's Hospital said, "People don't want to discuss bowels and livers over lunches and dinner parties or cocktails." He was right. The public awareness at that time was practically nil.

But Joe Segal could talk about it.

After explaining my hope to find a cure through research, Joe responded by saying that he would send us a contribution to our new volunteer foundation. Our first donation! As I left that great lunch with Joe Segal, I felt that I could walk on air! Joe and Rosalie continue their support for the CH.I.L.D. Foundation to this day and we are eternally grateful.

That first cheque from Joe Segal initiated the start of the CH.I.L.D. Foundation (The Foundation for Children with Intestinal and Liver Disorders) and resulted in the following:

A pediatric IBD research chair at UBC (a "first" in Canada);

A designated program for IBD at BC Children's Hospital;

Meaningful advice from the medical profession;

And yes! The first CH.I.L.D. Foundation Laboratory for Pediatric IBD Research in B.C.

Joe's business achievements are numerous and brilliant, and through all the 63 years of their marriage, Rosalie has been there to help and share his compassion for others. Their family – Sandra, Gary and Lorne – contribute their time by being involved in many good community causes, following the example of their parents.

Joe and Rosalie's grandchildren follow the family tradition even as young as they are and have committed themselves to "making a difference" in our work, just as their parents and grandparents before them.

Joe has made many decisions in his extraordinary business career, but his proposal of marriage to Rosalie was by far the best decision of his life. In their 63 years together, they have worked as a team and have seen times of modest means and many challenges.

For Rosalie and Joe, giving quietly to those in need is a way of life. They have together, and for over 60 years, always strived to help others.

CHAPTER 62

MARK GURVIS

CEO, Jewish Federation of Greater Vancouver

Joe Segal's leadership and philanthropic role in the Jewish community of the Lower Mainland spans such an extraordinary range of institutions, causes and projects it would be impossible to capture in a short "chapter" of this book. I'll therefore highlight one that I think is emblematic of his unique impact.

As the central fundraising and coordinating body of our local Jewish community, one of the Jewish Federation's key responsibilities is to inculcate the values and behaviours of giving and leadership in future generations. A few years ago, we undertook to introduce young adults who were starting to support our community on a meaningful level to some of the exemplary philanthropic leadership of our community, and to create opportunities for those veteran leaders to inspire by sharing their personal stories and reflections.

Among the natural first hosts, of course, were Joe and Rosalie Segal, who graciously agreed to have 60 young donors to their home. As part of that evening, Joe shared his story about how he got started in giving and community life.

It was a spellbinding evening as he talked about his modest roots in Vegreville, his army service and his beginning days in

Vancouver. His story demonstrated how throughout his life he has supported community, both inside and beyond the Jewish community, emphasizing the importance of taking care of those in need, and the importance of standing up and being counted.

What was most compelling for everyone who attended was how real Joe's emotion was as he talked with these young donors. I've been in enough meetings with Joe about enough issues and projects in our community to have seen his sharp mind at work, and his skillful navigation of a conversation to a result of his design. But I've also been privileged to see his true caring nature, and the emotional core of why he cares so deeply about so many important causes.

The evening that he hosted for our young donors was one of countless events that Joe and Rosalie have hosted for so many groups. But his openness and raw emotion that evening touched people, and provided them with exactly the kind of inspiration and example they were hoping for. It was a great example of what has made him such an extraordinary leader in the civic and philanthropic scene in the Lower Mainland.

CHAPTER 63

MEL COOPER C.M., O.B.C., LL.D.

Chair, TELUS Victoria Community Board

The Order of British Columbia, as readers may know, was established in 1989 to recognize those persons "who have served with the greatest distinction and excelled in endeavours benefiting others." The first recipients were so honoured in 1990.

Two years later, I met Joe Segal at the regal Government House in Victoria in a lineup of those who would be the 1992 honourees. We chatted about our wonderful province and our good fortune for having landed here – Joe from Alberta and I from Newfoundland. Little did either of us know we would have the opportunity to be of "significant service" to the province we now call home and to be described as "citizens dedicated to the betterment of British Columbia." We both agreed we considered serving beautiful B.C. as a privilege.

Conversation with Joe came easy. He was engaging . . . with a gentle smile that broke down any barriers that might exist between two strangers. Chatting for the first time, Joe had a twinkle in his eye. Twenty-one years later, he still does. I liked him from the start. For a man of considerable financial means, held in the highest regard by everyone who knows him, I thought to myself, 'He is truly modest.' As they would say in Newfoundland, "no airs about him."

And as my favourite aunt would add, "He doesn't fancy himself."

As we moved slowly towards the spacious, elegantly appointed ballroom where the Lieutenant Governor and the Premier of British Columbia would decorate 13 of us, Joe turned to me and whispered, "It's hard to believe that a boy from Vegreville, Alberta, and a boy from Signal Hill in St. John's would find themselves receiving the highest honour the province bestows." I said, "Yes, it's heady stuff, Joe." We entered into the elegant ballroom in alphabetical order. Joe and I had now parted.

Inside, some 175 people sat theatre-style, facing the stage, which was adorned with the Canadian and British Columbia flags and other regalia. They included family, friends, past recipients, political leaders, and the judges who had adjudicated the nominations and the required supporting letters. Soon, as the room went still, Michael Roberts, Secretary to Lieutenant Governor David Lam, walked to the microphone to welcome one and all to Government House and to ask us to stand for the arrival of His Honour. In the distance, we could hear the moaning sound of a bagpipe. The Pipe Major led the stage party into the ballroom. There's something about bagpipes that stirs you whether Jewish or Irish, like Joe and I. It's an emotional sound that Joe had heard for the first time and often after, as a member of the Calgary Highlanders during the Second World War. Joe and I are both compact people, but I swear we both felt taller at that moment.

Joe was the 12th person to receive the Order that April day. As his name was announced, I glanced around to see his loving lifelong partner, Rosalie, beam. Her pride and that of her attending family showed. I believe good things happen to good people. Joe has had many good things happen to him.

"We call Joseph Segal to come forward," said emcee Michael Roberts. Joe was led by a Government House attendant to the stage. Facing the audience, Joe heard emcee Roberts begin the citation, "Joseph Segal, an outstanding British Columbian and a Canadian merchandising legend, has given unstintingly of himself and his resources for the betterment of our province." ("How true," I said to myself). The audience listened intently as they were told of his arrival in Vancouver to open a small war-surplus clothing store ("I remember that little store in Pigeon Park on West Hastings Street." I heard myself thinking, 'Big trees from little acorns grow.').

The emcee continued with the amazing story of Joe, including his chain of 70 Fields Stores, the acquisition of Zellers and the day he became the largest single owner of Canada's iconic Hudson's Bay Company ('He's no ordinary Joe,' I thought). "Joseph Segal is a self-made entrepreneur whose legendary acumen and energies are turned as often to the needs of the community as to the demands of the executive suite," the emcee continued, describing Joe's endless "munificence" with many examples of his generosity. To conclude, emcee Roberts who had written these words himself, told the appreciative audience, "It has been said of Joseph Segal – if there is a good and noble cause, he is there."

Then the Lieutenant Governor, himself a much-admired philanthropist, placed the Order of British Columbia medal around Joe's neck. The medal depicts a stylish dogwood (the floral emblem of British Columbia) and features a crowned shield of arms. Joe smiled his warm smile. Then as Premier Mike Harcourt presented the Certificate of Appointment, the audience broke into sincere and lengthy applause of appreciation for his many contributions to others.

I thought to myself, 'I hope to get to know this man better one day.' I have. I've been present for many of his deserved recognitions and experienced numerous audience applauses since that first meeting in 1992.

Today, as one of our province's most decorated citizens, Joe continues to be a gentle, modest giant of a man. It is said, "You are known by the company you keep." To have been in his company as a friend over the last 21 years has only strengthened my admiration for Joseph Segal.

Munificent Joe.

CHAPTER 64

YITZCHAK WINEBERG

Rabbi, Chabad Lubavitch BC

Okay, so it's not "Lunch With Joe." I'm still waiting for Chartwell to go kosher!

Maybe it should be "Vodka With Joe." As many Sunday afternoons I have had the pleasure of spending time with Joe and Rosalie, and shared many a *L'Chaim* with him. But more than the drinks, it has to be the pleasure of his company. Insightful, humorous, caring, solicitous, empathetic and sympathetic.

In a world scarred by a lack of caring, someone who really cares stands out! To term Joe Segal a philanthropist would be too obvious a description. He donates to numerous charities, and is honoured and respected by so many. But frankly that's not what makes him unique. Yes, he is a success and yes, he gives back to his community. One would expect that, and indeed there are many like that (although Joe is a leader not a follower!).

Joe Segal is unique because of the individual caring and attention he (and Rosalie) give to those much less fortunate people. While others would consider them at best to be a nuisance, Joe embraces them! From ex-mental patients, down on their luck, ne'er-do-wells, down-and-out bums; they are welcome in his office and in his life. He gives not only of his money, but shares a quick joke, sagely advice, and often gives them a well-deserved lecture.

I have seen many charitable people in my almost 40 years as a serving Rabbi in the Vancouver community. We are indeed fortunate and blessed to have such a giving and magnanimous community. But try as I might, I can't find anyone who compares to Joe's (and Rosalie's) compassion, and indeed passion for giving.

These are not the recognized acts of charity. No plaques are presented; no honours are bestowed. They take up valuable time from a very hectic business day. Somehow, Joe finds time for everyone. Our holy Talmud teaches us that the act of charity is amply rewarded by the Almighty. But the act of charity that is accompanied by a smile, a kind word and sagely advice, is 11 times more valuable. I have personally witnessed the interaction between Joe and the people he helps quietly and privately. I can't help but be amazed!

Life is all about learning. We learn from our teachers, spouses, friends and even just the human experience. But there is no greater teacher, than one who sets an example by his or her conduct; and a standard that most can only be awed by it. Joe Segal is the consummate teacher! He has set a bar so high, that we can only admire and aspire to achieve.

May the Almighty continue to reward Joe and Rose with a long and meaningful life, good health, much *nachas* (pleasure) from their beautiful family, and most of all, a life that is filled with kindness and giving.

CHAPTER 65

CHIP WILSON

Founder & Chairman, Lululemon Athletica

It must have been 2007 and my company lululemon had just gone public. Even though I had been a Vancouverite for 20 years, to be invited to lunch with Joe Segal was unexpected. At my third lunch with Joe, he told me in a very matter-of-fact way that I was nervous with him. He was right. I held Joe in such high esteem, I now recognize I was trying to impress him. I wanted to be worthy of his time and mentorship.

What humoured me about Joe is that during each lunch, at some point he would get around to estimating my net worth and the cost of my house construction. Joe was never off by more than one per cent.

Joe is also what I would call a "good citizen" educator and he has coached me to give without expectation of return. He once told me about a woman who sent Rosalie a letter about her child's last days on earth and her desire to travel to complete a dream. Rosalie and Joe fulfilled that dream for a family that had no other resources.

Joe has always been clear about the fact that I should pass on 10 per cent of my yearly profits to charity. At first I thought it was a Catholic religious tithe, but then I remembered Joe is Jewish. I concluded that what Joe meant was a 10 per cent tithe was part of being a good member of the community. When my wife Shannon and I put a significant amount of money towards education in Ethiopia, Joe asked me if I wanted to be a small fish in the big pond of the world or a big fish in the small pond of Vancouver. It was a rhetorical question that didn't need a response. Joe just wanted me to think about it.

With charity, Joe told me, anyone can give money, but the real gift is time. Joe's coaching has made Shannon and me very cognizant of the balance between time and money. Now we make sure we are not giving money just to make ourselves feel good about not giving time.

Before we moved to Australia for a year, I had my last 2012 lunch with Joe. The lululemon stock value has increased enormously, due, I must say, not to me but to the incredible lululemon management. The last piece of advice I got from Joe was, "Once you are a billionaire, you never want to stop being a billionaire." This statement motivated me to diversify my portfolio, no matter how much I wanted to hold on to every lululemon share I held.

Thanks, Joe! Thanks for fighting for us in the Second World War. Thanks for the gambling stories and for the risk-taking that made you a great businessman. You are truly an icon to a whole country.

CHAPTER 66

PEETER WESIK

President, Wesgroup Properties

Lunch with Joe is never just lunch. When you first meet Joe, he wants to get to know you. He asks questions about your history, in a compassionate, caring way, that leads you to reveal the important things in your life that shaped who you are.

The topics at lunch cover the full array of social, political and economic issues. Joe is incredibly well read and informed. He brings a perspective to current issues that provide an insightful, thoughtful view, a wise view.

My first lunch with Joe was over 30 years ago, and I was invited as a guest. My friend who invited me was an energetic, focused, driven individual, who I thought was sure to succeed in life. The invitation to have lunch with Joe Segal was irresistible.

During lunch, my friend described his current projects and the dizzying pace of his life. I thought Joe would be impressed with my friend's energy and enthusiasm.

Joe then asked my friend about his family and how much time he spent with them, a question that 30 years ago was not much asked. Joe asked my friend if he was happy working so hard. And finally, Joe asked the question, "Are you sure you are being effective with your time? After all, we are given a limited amount of time in our lives."

That message has stayed with me all these years. And as the ultimate recognition of the impact Joe has had on a generation of business leaders in Vancouver, at a recent panel, senior business leaders were asked to comment on the important advice they had received during their careers. Without rehearsal, several leaders told stories of the important lessons they had learned in their lunches with Joe.

CHAPTER 67

RICK ILICH

President, Townline Homes Inc.

An interesting task, to write something about an industry icon who also happens to be a mentor and most importantly, a friend.

I have known Joe since I started working for Arthur and Henry Block under the stewardship of Jim Winton, the president of First National Lands and the Block Bros. Land Development Division.

In those days, my knowledge of Joe was more from the perspective of a rookie being moved up to the big leagues and having a periodic encounter with the seasoned pros.

This was the late '70s, a time when the banks accepted appraisal surplus as equity and 105 per cent financing was not unheard of... in essence, the good old days.

As the years passed and Joe continued to build his business and financial empire, Block Bros. came and went, as did Daon, First Capital, Imperial Ventures, NB Cook Corporation and many others. But Kingswood Capital just kept trucking. At the same time, Joe's influence on business and people grew so vast, I wouldn't doubt that the Grateful Dead's anthem, "Trucking," had Joe in mind when Jerry Garcia wrote it.

As years passed, Joe and my father, and ultimately, our families grew closer and closer. Although my dad's pride would not allow him to say it out loud, Joe had a very significant influence on my dad's business acumen and the growth of the business.

Like father, like son. My visits with Joe became more frequent over time and the more time I am given with Joe, the more I take something away, which has been beneficial in both my business and my personal life.

In the early years, our lunches started out with me pitching him on a deal, always looking for him to put up all the money, with the promise that, through my brilliance, I would deliver unbelievable returns.

Obviously, Joe saw right through my sales pitch, because he only invested once, and it was for a very short period of time. Joe has always had a keen sense for the deal. I regret not having heeded his advice in the early years as often as he offered it. I recall Joe saying on more than one occasion, "Rick, if it sounds too good to be true, it probably is." I was green enough at the time that it never occurred to me that he was really saying no to my "too good to be true" pitch.

A typical visit with Joe, usually started something like this, "Well Rick, what's cookin'? I see you have started on that Richmond site . . . that's a good deal, you should have come to me with that one. Well then, what are you drinking?"

"I think I will have red, they always have a decent Merlot here."

"Good idea . . . you know I only drink when I'm having lunch with you."

Over the next two or three glasses of wine or perhaps the

occasional martini, we cover business, usually my business, with a few questions thrown in about someone he is going to be meeting soon.

"What do you know about so-and-so?" he'll ask.

I always get a kick out of the "only drinking when he is with me" story. This time the young woman working in Yew comes up to the booth and says, "Look, Mr. Segal, we have Hendrick's in."

For a guy who infrequently partakes at lunch, his eyes sure light up and we both indulge in a couple of gin martinis. At this point, I understand that this is Joe's schtick and not my personal privilege.

Throughout many dozens of lunches that have covered business, family, life, some very sad times for both of us, some very good laughs and always ending with well-placed words of wisdom, I want to wrap this up with the most profound life lessons that Joe has passed on to me, spoken in Joe's own words:

"Rick, you've got your feet in two different boats, you're bound to wind up with a wet ass!"

"Rick, you've only got one ass, you can't ride two horses!"

And most importantly:

"Rick, you have to be happy to make a difference. You look happy now, you have pulled things together, you have a wonderful wife and family. Take good care of them and they will take care of you."

In the Buddhist faith, a spiritual leader or head of the temple is called the Rinpoche. If you are fortunate enough to have a Rinpoche read for you and offer you advice, it is a great privilege, but it takes a little bit out of the Rinpoche. Joe, I hope all of the advice I have walked away with from our lunches hasn't put too much of a strain on you because I have a lot more to ask, but please know that I have taken your advice and I have heeded your wisdom. Thank you for your mentorship and most importantly, thank you for your friendship.

CHAPTER 68

EVALEEN JAAGER ROY

Principal, Jaager Roy Advisory Inc.

Chair of the Board, Emily Carr University of Art & Design

How many of us can say we have a lifelong mentor?

That's what Joe Segal is for me.

We first met when I was just a kid, a student on the board of governors at Simon Fraser University. Somehow – how did I get so lucky? – we bonded and there began a rich and rewarding relationship. I got advice, encouragement, laughter and life philosophy, usually over lunch at Joe's special table at Chartwell and later Yew. For several wonderful years Joe and I ended up working together too, he as Chancellor of Simon Fraser University and me as the first alumni board chair.

Looking back, there are three priceless things that Joe taught me.

An unrelenting focus on excellence. An inherit belief that I could create anything I wanted in life. And most of all: the importance of giving. Not just giving monetarily – although we all know that Joe sets the bar for that, certainly in B.C. But more importantly, Joe taught me the importance of giving of oneself – to the community, to causes that matter, to people in need.

These values have shaped the woman I've become. And they are values that I convey to those I now mentor.

I can't resist ending with one of my favourite "Joe stories."

We all know that Joe is invariably happy and in a great frame of mind. But at one particular lunch many years ago, he was positively beaming. When I asked him why, he laughed and said, "What a great morning! We're doing a property review and I discovered that I own 200 acres of land in Ladner. I bought that land so long ago that I forgot about it!"

Well . . . Imagine forgetting you owned 200 acres somewhere! That day Joe and I celebrated by having a glass of champagne together. After all, who wouldn't, upon making such a fabulous discovery?

CHAPTER 69

JACQUI COHEN

President & CEO, Army & Navy Department Stores

Joe Segal . . . The BMOC, or in our language, the Big Macher, has always been there for the Cohen family. As a little "Pissher" in the world of retailing, I often sought out Joe's advice.

In the mid 1990s when I had just taken over the day-to-day operations at Army & Navy Department Stores, Joe and I had lunch. I was asking all sorts of questions like . . . who, what, where and when. Mr. Segal had a very stern expression on his face. He pointed his finger at me and said,, "Young lady, you're either in or you're out." I understood exactly what he meant.

A year or so later, we were once again breaking bread together and I was once again bending his ear. Joe strongly suggested that I do my due diligence on a property that Grandpa Sam had purchased in the 1940s in Port Coquitlam. Grandpa bought 12 acres of land to erect a sign advertising the Army & Navy in Vancouver and New Westminster, knowing how many cars would be driving by, heading west. Joe was well aware that by the '90s this strip of land was fast becoming the "Golden Mile" of the Dominion Triangle. It now sits smack between Walmart and Costco and is a future project for the Cohen family.

I have been extremely fortunate to have the ear and mentorship of Joe Segal.

CHAPTER 70

ERIC CARLSON FCA

CEO, Anthem Properties Group

I first met Joe Segal in 1997 when my company, Anthem Properties, entered into a contract with him to purchase 611 Alexander Street in Vancouver.

We loved the building that he had so gracefully converted from the American Can factory into a vibrant facility of designers, architects, schools and garment manufacturers. For a guy who was supposed to be a merchant, he certainly had an eye for design. Gastown, to this day, in 2013, is still catching up to what he originally recreated in the late 1980s.

As it turned out, we only purchased half the asset, as the transaction was a little bit too aggressive for us at that time, and we ran out of time before we could organize all of the financing necessary to complete the sale. Joe could have pushed us out of the deal. He had come to realize, over the contract period, that an emerging technology sector was providing renewed tenant interest, and that the income tax emanating from the sale was very high (those who know Joe understand that he never pays too much and he sells only if the price is favourable). He would have been better off not selling after all. The building was a keeper. But, being a reasonable man, and knowing how much we liked the building, he agreed to extend the closing and sell only half the building. We were both winners. And so it was and is with Joe, shrewd on the one hand, but going for a win/win on the other. What goes around, comes around.

Of course, that was only the beginning. I thought we were buying into real estate when we made that investment. Really, we got so much more. Both myself and my colleague David Ferguson took turns having lunch with Joe at the Four Seasons. First at Chartwell, then, after it closed, at Yew. Even though I was a serious young businessman ("lunch is for losers") and considered myself athletic and health conscious, I got caught up in the heavy wooden walls, rich food, strong martinis, heady conversation and Joe's alluring charm.

Through that lunch experience Joe would give and get, as he did with much of the younger generation of those years, gleaning information from enthusiastic associates, who were eager to please and participate. He would do math in his head, quickly and easily, as we talked about tenants, leases, deals and finance. He kept it simple and to the point. He could always pick a course of action. As he maintained the senior position in our partnership he led the charge. Dave and I used to joke that he was the best property manager we ever hired.

In addition to buying those special meals, he would offer advice, gently, and without us even realizing it.

"You work hard? Put in long hours? That's fine. That's what you need to do to get things done. But you are married, right? Do you do right by your wife? Do you love her? Do you tell her you love her? Eric, that's very important. I love my wife Rosalie as much, no more, than the day I first fell in love with her. All the money in the world means nothing without that." And there I would sit, having tried to play the game of high-powered lunch discussion, and he would take it, and me, right back to that basic fundamental place, of truth, honour and love, all in less than a minute, and without any heavy-handedness.

Other times he would encourage us to do more for our communities through charitable works and contributions: "Eric, you know the old saying, do unto others, as you would have them do unto you . . ."

Finally, there was and continues, his passion for life and for business. "Eric, I don't know if you know how much I am worth. It's not important (but it's a lot). I would give it all away. All of it. To get a chance to start again with nothing, provided I have the knowledge I have today. Life is just terrific . . ." or words to that effect.

Whether encouraging people to live up to their business potential, honour their family, support the community, or exude confidence in a happy and humble kind of way, Joe comes off as a good, kind and loving man. He is a class act.

It has been a privilege to know him.

CHAPTER 71

SHIRLEY BARNETT

Director, Dayhu Group of Companies

If I mention to a girlfriend that I am having lunch with Joe Segal, I inevitably get asked, "Aren't you intimidated by him?" No, I will answer. Why would I be? I have known Joe ever since I was nine years old and perhaps even before then.

Joe Segal is not only a friend, a mentor, an advisor, he is also a first cousin by marriage as my mother, Esther Dayson, and Rosalie's mother, Chava Wosk, were sisters. Rosalie was the flower girl at my parents' wedding and Joe was the master of ceremonies at mine. Our lives have been intertwined for years.

As I grew up and surfaced in the world of charity, luckily I developed a skill at knowing "who to call and for what." Joe saved me many phone calls. In 1979, when I decided to begin an interest-free lending society for poor people in the Jewish community, I called Joe. Not for money (I never call him for that), but because I knew he would intuitively understand the need. The cause would not require explanation, nor the significance it would have in the community. Joe just understood and he got it moving.

Joe does not serve on committees or non-profit boards yet he can read their financials in seconds, analyze their situation in minutes and develop a strategic plan for them shortly after.

His thoughts are "big picture" but his actions are immediate and decisive. Whether it is the Jewish community, United Way, mental health or the Downtown Eastside, he "gets it." How does he do this? Yes, he is smart, but there are lots of smart people. It's more than that. It is intuition layered on top of reason, intellect and curiosity.

Why is the Joe I know so unique? First of all, he reads everything that is sent to him and he remembers everything that he reads. That in itself is annoying to us ordinary folks. Secondly, he is fascinated by all kinds of people and his curiosity about them quickly turns to caring.

Now let's talk about Joe the flirt – yes, he is! – but that's all part of his charm.

No matter what the topic has been at lunch, he will always say, "So . . . is there a man in your life?" When I reply no (as I generally do!), he always hits me with, "You're too fussy. What are you looking for?"

My answer is always the same: "Actually, Joe, I'm looking for someone like you . . . only 10 years younger!"

Joe, as always, thanks for lunch and for so much more.

CHAPTER 72

PETER ARMSTRONG ICD.D

Executive Chairman & Founder, Rocky Mountaineer

You can't think of Joe Segal without thinking about his family. For me, I was always so impressed with how Joe involved his family from an early age in all of his activities, be it business, philanthropy, religion or community – his family was always with him. Of course, his wonderful wife Rosalie is his biggest supporter and his rock. His two sons, Gary and Lorne, have helped Joe expand his reach.

I got to know Joe through his philanthropy. On numerous times I was invited to Joe and Rosalie's home for charity functions. I also had the pleasure of being with Joe on the Vancouver Police Foundation Board.

However, the most important interaction I had with Joe was when he was a judge in the Ernst & Young Entrepreneur of the Year Award. I was nominated. I didn't really understand the process but went to all the different events, including the gala dinner. Our company was well profiled and while I was anxious (and a bit competitive!), I wanted to win. I didn't win. Another well-deserving individual and firm did. I was a bit crestfallen. When leaving the dinner at the end, and busy congratulating people, Joe came through the crowd and said, "I want to talk to you. You've got a great story. You've got a great company. You will win someday –

you know that. Just keep working at it and we'll see you up there on the stage." With that, he turned and walked away. Wow! In my mid-30s to have Joe Segal tell me I was going to be a success made me feel, really, really good. I actually did win that night! Not the prize I thought I would win; however, the prize I needed to win!

Joe touches so many people and for that brief moment he taught me a lot about being tenacious and not giving up. Years later, I did win and I will forever credit Joe for doing what's more important – showing someone who competed that they are doing well, even without winning. Joe is a great mentor.

CHAPTER 73

JACK P. BLANEY

President Emeritus, Simon Fraser University

It is not at all an exaggeration to say that the character of downtown Vancouver and the culture of Simon Fraser University were shaped in important ways by lunch with Joe Segal.

In 1981, I left Joe's office without the gift I had in mind (look, I was an amateur then) but I did leave convinced that Joe Segal would be a huge asset to SFU's board of governors. The then-SFU president George Pedersen persuaded Joe to join the board and thus began Joe's long relationship with SFU as board member, university chancellor and steadfast friend.

At our very first lunch Joe expressed amazement that SFU was built on a mountain when UBC was far from the city's centre. Canada's foremost retailer questioned why we appeared so uninterested in being closer to our customers or in strengthening our competitive position. I loved it.

Joe's lunch table soon became command centre central as we sought to establish a downtown campus in the right place (street level, city core, public transit) at the right price (as close to free as possible).

In early discussions, Joe was perplexed that SFU's faculty was far from unanimous in its support for a downtown campus.

A core of faculty was so opposed that more staff time went into securing campus support than went into assisting Sam Belzberg to raise money for the campus. Critical to the successful outcome was that Joe could directly engage opposing faculty at board of governors meetings.

Just blocks from Joe's first Hastings Street store, the university in 1989 opened SFU at Harbour Centre – the beginning of an ever-growing downtown Vancouver presence for the university. Other post-secondary institutions followed. Mayors Gordon Campbell and Philip Owen acclaimed SFU's commitment to be "in and of the city." Joe was their hero.

At a particularly pivotal lunch, Joe considered Peter Eng's offer to give SFU the former TD Bank building, at Seymour and Hastings, so that the university could create a unique conference centre that would epitomize a perfect place for dialogue. Joe's conclusion was that the centre would be a "jewel in the city." That declaration confirmed its feasibility and energized our team. Joe chaired the centre's fundraising council and, as he had done with Harbour Centre, captained the closing deal.

Joe begins lunch with, "Well, what's new?" This really is code for, "What have you accomplished since we last met?"

Small lunch. Big ideas. Things happen.

CHAPTER 74

DAVID McLEAN

Chairman, The McLean Group

My friend and neighbour Joe Segal is always there when you need some advice. We have had numerous lunches at the Four Seasons where I have sought his counsel and wisdom.

I remember one particular lunch about 20 years ago. We were involved in a deal with a Toronto-based life insurance company. There was a drop in the Toronto real estate market and the investors in the fund they set up were demanding to be cashed out.

We had done a deal with them on a convertible debenture where after five years they could convert it to equity. They called and said they needed to raise the cash, could we cash them out? Of course we could, but we would want a discount. But how much should we ask for?

They had $18 million in the dealing including principal and accrued interest. I thought we would offer to cash them out for $14 million, a little less than a 25 per cent discount.

So I called Joe – we had lunch and I told him my story. He took out his pad and wrote down a few numbers then he said to offer them $7 million. I said I can't do that; they will never accept it. He smiled and said, "You have to learn how to negotiate. They badly need the cash, you have the cash and you do not have to buy them out – offer them $7 million."

We flew to Toronto and met with them in their highrise office downtown. We talked and I told them how tough it was to raise cash, but we have an offer. He said, "How much?" And with a straight face I said, "Seven million." He went apoplectic! It is too low – you must think we are crazy. I said that is our offer – call me tomorrow.

The phone rang early the next morning. He wanted $10 million. I knew now Joe was right, and we settled for $8.5 million. Joe's advice had made us $5.5 million – a 53 per cent discount!

What a great friend.

CHAPTER 75

GORDON R. DIAMOND LL.D., O.B.C.

Chairman, West Coast Reduction Ltd.

"Lunch With Joe" conjures up many happy memories of the days when my father and I were in business together. In those days we often took our customers to lunch at Chartwell in the Four Seasons Hotel, and one thing we could always count on was seeing Joe sitting at his corner table surveying all around him. In an uncertain world, Joe's inevitable presence at his table on any day of the week was a reassuring sight.

Sometimes, Joe did us the honour of inviting us to join him for lunch with his select group of guests. More often than not, however, we arrived with guests of our own, and it was these occasions I particularly remember for, invariably, when we arrived at Chartwell, we would go over to Joe's table where we would greet each other and exchange pleasantries.

Being curious men, both my father and Joe literally itched to find out who their respective guests were and what business was being transacted.

Knowing Joe's interest had been piqued by my father's arrival at the restaurant, not to mention that my father was equally interested in Joe's guests, I often visited Joe at his table at the end of lunch and smilingly expressed my regret at the fact that we had been unable to include him in the business that had just been transacted with our guests. I am sure that Joe knew that our guests were mainly meat packers, pork processors, chicken processors and fish processors, but we both took delight in ribbing each other about opportunities discussed and deals made.

My father and Joe had great respect for one another and it is probably true to say that Joe looked upon my father, Jack Diamond, as a mentor.

It is no coincidence, however, that Joe has gone on to become a businessman with few peers and one of Canada's leading philanthropists. However, without the enduring support of his wife Rosalie, it is unlikely Joe would have attained the heights he has reached.

It is a privilege for Leslie and me to know Joe and Rosalie and their family, and to count them all among some of our most honoured friends.

CHAPTER 76

RYAN BEEDIE

President, Beedie Development Group

Although I have only known Joe for a few years, he has had a significant impact on me and my perspective on philanthropy.

The first time I had lunch with Joe, he was able to accurately calculate (in his head) the approximate net cash flow from the leasing side of our business. His ability to process information and summarize things in a timely manner is beyond impressive. He went on to outline his philosophy saying something to the effect of "you pay the bank, you pay yourself something to live a comfortable life and the rest is extra for giving away." It was Christmastime during the economic meltdown of 2008 and we were talking about how fortunate we are and how important it is to always think of others. During our conversation we talked about how many families were struggling and we agreed to each make a significant contribution to the Food Bank.

In subsequent meetings and lunches, we continued discussing these themes and Joe encouraged me to think bigger, opening my mind to bigger opportunities for giving. There is no doubt that Joe was a huge inspiration for our gift to SFU that created the Beedie School of Business (which includes the Segal Graduate School). Words cannot describe how wonderful it feels to be able to make such an enduring gift. I am grateful for this every day and thank Joe for encouraging me to do this. Had it not been for Joe, this would not have happened.

Joe has told me that it is possible for me to become one of the city's largest benefactors. While I do not know if this is true, this encouragement adds further motivation for me to be successful so that I am in an even better position to "do good" and "give back."

The time Joe has taken as a mentor to me (and so many others) speaks volumes about him. Not only is he generous financially, he is equally generous with his time. When students and others approach me for advice, I am happy to give the time because it is what Joe did. I want to make Joe proud.

CHAPTER 77

DARREN CANNON

Executive Vice President, Colliers International

I always look forward to my lunches with Joe – I wish there were more of them. I walk back to my office inspired and regenerated, sometimes chuckling to myself on the short 10-minute walk. Joe entertains from the time he sits down. Endless people stop by the table and he always remembers their names, makes a wisecrack and then the coveted grin.

The first question he always asks me is what I think the cap rate for Kingswood is. This is the highest-quality logistics-based business park in the city. Pension funds salivate over it – but Joe knows all this. After playing into his hand over a countless number of lunches, I finally became smart last year. When he asks, I always tell him 500 bps higher than he wants to hear. He looks at me with a puzzled look and says, "Are you crazy? It's a 4.5 cap and I have an offer sitting on my desk – what should I do?" Whatever I say, he always replies, "I wouldn't sell it!"

I remember one time JS was giving my colleague and me relationship advice. My buddy had just been dumped by his girlfriend and was shattered. He didn't tell Joe she had broken up with him but asked for his advice and described the girl. Joe said, and I quote, "If you love her, don't let her go." What Joe didn't know is she had let him go and was running for the hills. That was the icing on the cake.

At an ensuing lunch with my wife, she was asking Joe about relationships. He quickly told her, "If you want chicken soup, you have to put a chicken in the pot!" In other words, we all have to contribute in our relationships, our workplace and in the community.

Every deal I conclude for Joe ends with him calling me. Not to tell me he is happy or thanking me for a job well done but to ask me how big of a cheque I am sending over for the charity of his choice.

Joe is the most gracious and giving person I know. But it's the entertaining and insightful lunches that are ingrained in me. Joe will always be my favourite client and friend to lunch with. Maybe this is why he always gets a break on fees!

CHAPTER 78

FRED WRIGHT FCA

Chair, Capital West Partners

I was first introduced to Joe Segal 43 years ago at the age of 29 by my boss, John Chaston, a director of Fields Stores and chief executive officer of investment bank Pemberton Securities. Joe was a valued Pemberton client and I was assigned to do his bidding.

In the fray on most Joe-inspired initiatives, most notably the Fields-Zellers-Hudson's Bay chain of events, I always marvelled at the ease with which Joe, with patience, magnetic charm, sincere interest in people and profound common sense, continually converted his toughest adversaries. Little wonder then, that when Pemberton went public in 1986, as chief executive officer, I nominated Joe to become the first independent director of Pemberton in more than 100 years of doing business.

And so it happened that in 1976, on the cusp of a landmark decision, emotions were running amok at Montreal-based Zellers' special shareholders' meeting. Distraught in extremis, shareholders were being asked to turn over their keys to new boss-to-be Joe Segal, a relative stranger in Central Canada. The target of much verbal abuse, Joe listened attentively but remained stoically calm. During the meeting and thereafter, I marvelled at Joe's supreme calm and only years later came to understand that his calm was much less a matter of stoicism than it was of a bone-deep belief in the power of his idea.

Joe understood from Fields' success that his customers, quite simply, wanted quality merchandise at attractive prices. And Joe knew how to deliver it to them at a tidy profit. In what was an early articulation of retail colossus Costco's credo, Joe explained, "At Fields we're not running a stereotype department store that offers a full range in all departments. This operation is more a mix in constant change depending on the availability of merchandise that our customers want."

Predictably, Joe prevailed at the Zellers meeting. Thereafter, in two short years he energized Zellers, sold it and Fields to Hudson's Bay and became the Bay's largest shareholder before moving on to create his second colossus, a burgeoning real estate empire, based most certainly, on the amazing strength of an idea.

CHAPTER 79

JACK McGEE CD, LL.D. (Hon)

Former President, Justice Institute of British Columbia

"You must get to know Joe Segal," recommended the late Stan Hagen, an MLA and cabinet minister in the B.C. provincial government. To me, Stan was a friend and mentor from when I commanded Canadian Forces Base Comox. His advice was welcome as I prepared to be president of the Justice Institute of British Columbia.

"Joe Segal just completed six years as Chancellor of Simon Fraser University and 12 years on its board, he knows post-secondary education very well and is a highly influential business and community leader. He will have some good advice for you." Stan was right.

For 20 minutes, Dr. Joseph Segal politely listened to me describing the Institute and its importance to public safety. His questions and comments reflected his business acumen. "Why would someone want to support the JIBC? It does government work. The JIBC story has to appeal to the audience, the person being addressed. Focus on the programs and their value to the community." Joe's comments were kept in mind as the JIBC evolved, providing pathways from its renowned training courses to new, high-quality undergraduate and graduate-level programs and applied research, expanding the global reach and reputation of the Institute.

Lunch with Joe at Yew Restaurant is enlightening – an opportunity to benefit from his insights and vision and meet other leaders who would drop by to converse with him about business or community matters. As he came to know the JIBC, Joe acknowledged, "I didn't realize the strength of the Institute or the contribution it made to society. The Institute has to be recognized, it has to be better known. It deserves a higher profile; more penetration in the community." In his view, the Justice Institute is a "University for Life" because of the role of its graduates – emergency responders, counsellors and conflict resolvers – professionals providing "primary defence for everyone in the community."

Joe is well known for his and his family's philanthropy. At the JIBC, the Joseph and Rosalie Segal Award supports social workers studying complex trauma and child abuse, and aboriginal learners. Joe told recipients, "It is gratifying and heart-warming that you have seized the opportunity our fund provides to pursue a career that is important to you and to society." To the audience he emphasized the importance of giving to students who need community support to achieve their career goals.

When Joe learned I was retiring, he counselled, "Don't retire, don't be a schmuck! Continue to be involved, continue to learn: do meaningful activities, be vital. You only have so many days on earth, use them wisely and well." Sage advice reflecting Joe's philosophy of "the runway of life" amplified by Peter Legge in his book of that name.

I feel fortunate and grateful to know Joseph Segal. He is an inspiration, a man of upstanding character, an exemplar in business and community leadership who finds great pleasure in helping others achieve their education, career and life goals.

CHAPTER 80

GREG SPRUNG

Executive Vice President, Banking, Canadian Western Bank

I don't remember the date but I remember the day. I was leading a team of commercial bankers, relatively new to the job, but I was certainly aware of who Joe Segal was from my previous role in the bank's credit department. Linda Webb, who was Joe's relationship manager, decided it was time for me to meet and have lunch with Joe.

We arrived at Chartwell at noon sharp and were shown to a somewhat conspicuous round table in the upper corner of the restaurant. We were informed where to be seated, which took into consideration where Joe normally sits. As this was my first time, the 'tradition' was new to me; so, I was in training. At 12:15, an impeccably dressed gentleman entered the restaurant; after several stops shaking hands and meeting people at the tables that were on the way, he came to our (I mean Joe's) table.

After the normal pleasantries, something happened; we got along famously. Joe was warm, friendly and shared his thoughts on the real estate market, the importance of good service (especially from the bank) and a myriad of other topics. I could tell right away that if I was looking for good advice, this is where I would find it. When lunch was finished, I wanted to do it again, and soon. Did I mention the martini and glass of red wine?

So began my relationship with Joe. Lunches, many; advice, always; friendship for life over the next 20 years. We've had many business dealings together, participated in philanthropic causes and most importantly, Joe has made me feel like part of the Segal family. Through Joe, I have met many people and he has always been very supportive and an advocate of the institutions where I have worked. Whenever our senior people needed advice on the economy, markets or real estate in B.C., where would I take them? To see Joe, of course.

Several years ago, I was approached to consider a new challenge for the balance of my working career. At the time I was happy where I was, but after much thought and internal conflict, was considering a change. At lunch, Joe looked at me and said, "Greg, you can't ride two horses with one ___." I will let you fill in the blank. I was astounded as I had not made any decision but somehow, he knew there was unrest in my mind. He has ways of knowing these things. I made up my mind the next day and the rest is history.

Recently I was promoted, and during the period pending the announcement, I felt the need to let Joe know. He was in Hawaii, and Rosalie answered the phone; we chatted. Joe came to the phone, probably thinking there was something wrong. I informed him of my promotion and thanked him, as it was his fault. All the support and advice he gave me over the years helped make this possible, not to mention the two-horses thing. He was very gracious; even suggested I might have had something to do with it. That's Joe!

As I write this and obviously thinking about Joe, and of course, Rosalie, his family and all they have accomplished (far from finished yet; just ask), I look forward to our lunch at Yew next Thursday at noon; 12:15 his time, and wonder about the advice he will share.

Thank you, Joe, for your mentorship and friendship.

CHAPTER 81

RON EMERSON

President, Emerson Real Estate Group

The first time I met Joe Segal or became aware of Joe was back in 1974. I had arrived in Vancouver from Australia and was invited to attend a company Christmas party by a young lady that I had met. It turned out that the company was Fields Stores and the Christmas party was at the Coach House in North Vancouver. I think there were probably about 500 people at the function and I will never forget watching this individual working his way around to every table in the room. It was Joe Segal greeting each of his employees and their guests. When he came to our table he knew the names of every Fields employee at that table. At that time I had no idea that I would come to know Joe in the future; however, I was so impressed that the owner of the company would take the time to wish everyone the best and that he knew the names of all of the employees.

Joe is a wonderful person who has done incredibly well; however, he is the same individual that I first encountered back in 1974. He is a very humble person, extremely intelligent and very generous. Joe's son Lorne came to work at A.E. LePage where I worked and through that connection, I met Joe and ended up having a Monday-morning telephone call with Joe for many years.

Joe had many great sayings that I have been privy to hearing over the years, and the extent of his wisdom is hard to believe. For real estate Joe would say, "You make your money when you buy, not when you sell." Very simple but also very true.

Joe is one of the very few individuals in the world who is able to look at things and see them in black or white. This allows him to make decisions and not second-guess himself. Very few people have this quality and I believe it is the single most significant factor that allows very successful people to achieve their success.

Another one of Joe's favourite expressions is "there are no miracles." I believe that Joe is a miracle given the success he has had and continues to have and the time and money that he gives back to the community. Joe gives a lot of money to the various charities and causes in the city, but I know he also gives money and help to many individuals privately, for which he seeks no recognition.

I have never met a person with a memory like Joe's. In downtown Vancouver he can go up and down Howe and Hornby streets where Pacific Centre is located and name all of the businesses that were located there prior to the assembly and construction of Pacific Centre. His memory and ability to calculate complex numbers in his mind makes him a master negotiator. Joe has taught me that you must do your homework and be prepared for a negotiation well in advance. He is the best negotiator I have ever met and can conclude a negotiation where he gets where he wants to be and the other party feels they have been successful also. Joe is very fair and treats people with respect.

I feel very privileged to have the relationship I have with Joe and to have been involved in many deals over the past 30 years. I am honoured to be asked to contribute to this book and send to Joe and Rosalie my best wishes.

CHAPTER 82

MARSHALL CRAMER

Past President at Tahari, Jones New York and Christian Dior
Owner, Kaplan's Star Deli

Oh, to have known Joe Segal, both professionally and personally for over 20 years and be asked to pen one chapter in Peter Legge's book: impossible. Twenty chapters, maybe. One chapter, three days of intense mind editing. The quest would be to focus on an aspect of Joe's daily acumen that would show a different side, something beyond his knowledge, his keen business mind, his many friendships, his mentorship and his philanthropy.

I first met Joe in May of 1991 by phone, Joe in Vancouver and me in New York City. The memory still brings a smile. I arrived home in Connecticut from my day in New York City. The phone rings at about 9 p.m. and the voice on the other end announces that he is Joseph Segal from Vancouver, British Columbia. Joe proceeds to ask me how the weather is in New York. It happened to have been an unusual May and temperatures were already in the 90s and humid. Joe responded by saying that it was 70 degrees in Vancouver with no humidity, would I consider moving to British Columbia? No, thank you, Mr. Segal, I love it here in New York, especially on Seventh Avenue. We spoke for a while about the industry, exchanged thank-you's and disconnected. That disconnect lasted for exactly 24 hours. At 9 p.m. the following night, the phone call was again from Joe. The conversation was consistent with the previous night, including Vancouver weather conditions and forecasts that remained fabulous. These calls continued on most weekday nights and occasional Sundays for weeks. Well into June, New York remained hot and humid, while Vancouver was dry and perfect.

Weeks into these continuous calls, Joe informed me that he had to travel to Toronto and would I consider flying up to meet him for dinner. As fate would have it, I was scheduled to be there to launch a Canadian subsidiary. Joe probably already knew that. A terrific dinner at Il Posto and a wonderful evening of conversation followed. What a charming gentleman! My answer remained a consistent "no" to queries about my interest in moving. The calls did not abate. By July, my wife Sally knew Joe as well as I did and had never met him.

As summer progressed, the conditions in New York remained meteorically oppressive while Vancouver became the new San Diego in my mind, based on Joe's weather reports. What a paradise. Early August, Joe invited Sally and myself to a weekend in paradise. Why not? — we had never been north of Seattle. We arrived for the B.C. Day long weekend. It rained for four days. "Very usual," says Joe, but "isn't it a beautiful city?" Somewhere through the clouds I guess it was. We met the entire Segal family that weekend and we bonded instantly. However, an offer to move to Vancouver, to accept the presidency of Mr. Jax, was again gratefully declined. Tuesday I was back in sweltering and humid

New York City. Tuesday evening, at home, the phone again rang at 9 p.m. "How's the weather in New York? It's beautiful here in Vancouver . . . sunny, clear and dry."

After another dinner in Toronto during September, along with Morley Koffman and Dan Pekarsky, both board members of Mr. Jax, I finally relented and moved to Vancouver on October 31. Boy, did it rain in November of that year and every year thereafter.

The relationship with Joe and Rosalie and the family has continued and has developed into the fabric of our family here in Vancouver.

Two interesting things about Joe Segal: his intense focus on accomplishing what he sets out to do and, most importantly, it's always sunny, warm and clear in Vancouver.

CHAPTER 83

BILL FOX

President, Ledcor Properties Inc.

I first had the pleasure of meeting Joe Segal when an affiliate of our company was interested in purchasing a piece of property in downtown Vancouver that Joe owned. They asked me to approach Joe on their behalf to see if he would consider selling the property.

At the time, Joe was already legendary for his many deals, such as the purchase and sale of Zellers and the Bay. The prospect of negotiating with him – one of the most successful self-made Canadian businessmen ever – was a bit intimidating. I wasn't sure if he would even take my call so that I could at least explain the deal, or if I would just be passed on to an employee who would tell me the property wasn't for sale. Much to my surprise, I got through to Joe on my first attempt to call, and he was very interested in finding out why we would want to purchase that particular piece of property. As I expected, he told me the property wasn't available, but he did ask me to drop in so that he could see what we were planning and perhaps talk about selling or establishing a partnership.

That initial call launched a few meetings to discuss the deal, but more importantly it led to a friendship built over several wonderful lunches at the Four Seasons, where he had a special table always waiting for him. How fortunate I was to spend time with this very engaging, wise and philanthropic man!

Lunch with Joe was always entertaining. Over a glass wine, which he always enjoyed, he introduced me to many interesting people who would stop by to say hello, and he never shied away from giving advice, generously offering his insight and always remaining positive. He liked to joke with the waitresses, suggesting they should be married and having kids, or if they were already married, then he would proclaim in his fatherly way, "Okay then; you better take care of each other and your kids!"

His consistent message to me reflected the way he lived his own life: "Bill, you've got to give back to your community, to help others."

Thanks to Joe, I usually came away from our lunches feeling more upbeat and more knowledgeable about the real estate market, but more importantly, I left feeling a little more humble and with a better perspective on what's most important in life.

CHAPTER 84

MSGR. FREDERICK M. DOLAN

Vicar, Opus Dei Canada

The regulars at Yew Restaurant must have all sorts of reactions when they see Joe hosting a Catholic priest for lunch. My guess is that some are curious, others bewildered, but nobody is surprised. Joe's openness and zest for life is the stuff of legend.

The highlight of my visits to Vancouver is always spending time with Joe. Faith is the inevitable topic of our wide-ranging conversations. His insatiable appetite for exploring the deepest facets of human experience is a sign of his youthful mind.

My treasured friendship with Joe has led to important friendships with Rose, Gary and Nanci, Lorne, and Joe's grandson Justin. Thanks to those relationships, I have been graced with meeting Dr. Rick Hodes and learning about his remarkable work in Africa.

During one of our luncheons, Joe learned of a project in which I am involved: building a conference and retreat centre in Britannia Beach. Not only did Joe pose many interested questions, but he went to great lengths to put me in contact with someone whose help proved to be decisive.

Just thinking of the panoply of stories that will make up *Lunch With Joe* gives me great pleasure. What a fitting testimonial to a gentleman who has lived life so very well.

CHAPTER 85

KENNETH W. MAHON BCom, FCA

Chairman, Adera Group of Companies

My lunches with Joe occurred in the early 1980s when we had 22 per cent interest rates and plummeting real estate values. Joe and I had a few things in common in that we both owned large tracts of land in Richmond and had a number of mutual friends in the real estate business (Milan Ilich, Michael Audain, Ron Emerson), so we had lots to talk about.

Joe passed on knowledge largely through storytelling and he had lots of stories of the business deals and the banking and financing arrangements that he was able to work. I mostly listened and gained much knowledge from Joe.

I learned that you can never have enough cash because no one wants to lend you cash when things are tight like they were in the early 1980s. That one piece of advice has stood me and our group of companies in good stead, as we have been able to weather a number of storms over the years and come out the other end a bit bent, but not broke.

It was always difficult to pay for lunch when you lunched with Joe. The surest way, I found, was to give the head waiter a credit card on arrival and insist on the charge being put on that card. We have maintained contact over the years and have enjoyed many evenings at Rosalie and Joe's lovely home, which they generously donate for charity events. A great couple who have made many fine contributions to our community over the years.

CHAPTER 86

BRITTA BENNEKOU

Executive Assistant to Joseph Segal, Kingswood Capital Corporation

The first time I met Joseph Segal was in an interview to become his executive assistant. I left his office that day, after being put in the hot seat (a worn-out spot on the orange couch where many have sweated before me!), absolutely sure that I did not get the job. He didn't want to know about my work background at all; he wanted to know *who* I was, where I grew up, what my parents did, who I was married to, etc. – and in the space of 15 minutes he managed to make me blush, stammer and blurt out all my secrets! Now, after more than five years as his EA, I know that is his usual approach. Mr. Segal is curious – curious about everyone and everything. He wants to know what makes people tick. He values authentic experiences, getting to know people intimately and hearing their real life story – he is a true study of human nature.

JS (as he's affectionately called around here) is forever learning. He reads six newspapers every single morning before work! Here is a man who did not finish high school, yet knows a tremendous amount about the world, commerce and real estate. He can read financial statements like a CA, skim through proposals quickly and pick out a gem, and year after year, makes incredible real estate deals that outrageously tend to double once he owns them.

I marvel at Mr. Segal's stamina and grace. At 88, he comes to work each day in a custom-tailored suit and tie, with a monogrammed JS on his sleeve, and with the Order of B.C. and the Order of Canada flowers pinned on his lapel. He still takes several daily appointments, punctuated by a noon lunch meeting at the Four Seasons' Yew restaurant (where he has dined daily since 1979). After work, a session with his personal trainer; then more often than not, he must attend a formal soiree of some sort, nearly every night . . . a schedule that would exhaust a man half his age.

JS mentors more people than I can count, and takes practically every appointment asked of him. He is accessible to all and wants to share his time to lend sound advice or a helping hand. They say that if you spend time with successful, entrepreneurial types, that's what you'll become – and this is true for me so far. While working for him, I have sold two homes and bought three. I will be forever grateful for the real estate and investing wisdom he has shared with me.

Mr. Segal is literally asked for thousands of dollars each week by all manner of organizations, charities and individuals, and he is extremely generous. I know he wishes he could fund them all, and feels frustrated when he must decline. But he doesn't suffer fools lightly – and is good at sniffing out the frauds. Suffice it to say, while under his employ I have learned a lot of Yiddish words such as nudnik, schmuck, meshugener and schmo! One of my favourite expressions about life from JS is, "You can't ride two horses with one ass – choose the horse you want to ride or you'll fall through the cracks!" Stellar advice, no?

CHAPTER 87

JOSEPHINE M. NADEL

Barrister & Solicitor, Owen Bird Law Corporation

I have known Joe and Rosalie and their family since I was about six years old, having been a classmate and friend of Gary's since that time. I have known them from both a family and community perspective. They are pillars of our community and are exemplary in upholding the values of family and philanthropy. I would say that Joe has worked tirelessly for many decades to create security for his family while cultivating and deepening his service to those less fortunate. Joe epitomizes Sir Winston Churchill's adage that "we make a living by what we get and we make a life by what we give."

Joe has many striking attributes. Among those that I find truly inspirational:

Integrity: Joe's word is his bond; his handshake more credible than the most artfully crafted legal contract.

Leadership: Joe is a leader who has a clear vision and objective sense of what needs to be accomplished. He takes responsibility. Joe follows through and follows up. He holds others accountable to the standards he sets for himself.

Courage: Joe is not driven by fear or self-doubt. He is confident and surefooted and has the courage of his convictions.

If Joe has a secret weapon, I believe it is his sheer intellectual ability, his brainpower. He sees the forest, he sees the trees. He is analytical. His mathematical abilities are legendary. What he lacks in formal academic training, he has gained in the "university of life" and I can only presume that much has been self-taught.

It has been an honour to witness these qualities firsthand.

Joe's "door is open" to those in need of support, guidance, advice and mentorship. For me, personally, Joe has supported and encouraged me in reaching my goals whether it was the "Women on Board" Mentoring Program, an appointment to the board of a highly respected foundation or my legal career.

Joe's life experiences have been motivators, not deterrents or impediments. What might have been setbacks for some – humble beginnings, loss of his father at a young age, Second World War combat – were springboards for Joe to achieve a life of meaning.

Joe, if life is a runway, then you are a most distinguished and exemplary pilot of a state-of-the-art aircraft.

CHAPTER 88

HOWARD A. BLANK

Vice President, Corporate Communications, Entertainment & Responsible Gaming, Great Canadian Gaming Corporation

In September 2005, I was hosting a gala event at the River Rock Show Theatre as part of the opening-month launch of the spectacular new resort and casino.

My role was to be the gala auctioneer and co-master of ceremonies for the David Foster Foundation Gala, a benefit helping organ transplant and research in Canada.

Canada's own David Foster was present as were a bevy of stars and a 1,000-seat packed audience of a who's who of finance, philanthropy, the arts, science and media.

I was nervous as I stepped out on stage and began my schtick to raise funds for one-of-a-kind experiences and items.

Following my presentation, a man came up to me and gave me a warm handshake and asked who I was. I said my name and the man instantly asked if Hymie Blank was my grandfather. I replied yes and the most magnificent conversation ensued with Joe Segal telling me about how my grandfather sold "shmatas" (clothing) to him and how my grandfather, whom I never met, was a kind and great man.

Mr. Segal also asked about me and found out that I work for Great Canadian Gaming Corporation. He said, "You've missed your calling" as an MC and comedian. I replied that perhaps this is just the beginning for me and he encouraged me to keep at it, as it is a wonderful feeling to give back to the community.

Mr. Segal's words resonated with me. I honed my craft on stage and today I MC and celebrity-auctioneer at and for over 100 events per year. I volunteer for and sit on many philanthropic boards including: Variety, Honour House, Special Olympics BC, Odd Squad, C.H.I.L.D. Foundation, Grey Cup and Chabad of Vancouver.

Mr. Segal encouraged me to give back and grow as a citizen of this province and he has always been there at events and functions to encourage me and applaud my work volunteering to make our community a better place. I owe Joseph Segal so much for encouraging me and for following me in my philanthropic endeavours. Mr. Segal is a giant of a man, a father, a grandfather and a humanitarian. I am honoured to call him a friend and through our relationship, I have formed a deep friendship with his son Lorne, and I have now collaborated with Lorne on Coast Mental Health's Courage to Come Back Awards and other events for which he is responsible in Vancouver.

Joseph Segal has given me the spark to reach for my dreams while also giving back along the way. His commitment to philanthropy is something we all should emulate.

CHAPTER 89

KELLY S. HEED

Vice Chairman, Colliers International

Lunch with Joe was such a treat but one of the prerequisites was that you better have a fresh piece of information to share. If he hadn't heard it, you were safe. I've always called Joe my hero because he could outpace most everyone irrespective of age. A lot of lunches would start with him asking a question like: Have you tried Hendrick's gin? I'd say no, but if you're having it, I'm having it because you're my hero. Then the question on the wine and my same answer.

I often took one of our younger brokers who was keen to meet Joe and they would start by mentioning how much they admired what he had accomplished. Joe would quickly respond by saying that he would trade positions with them. What Joe meant was that he would not only trade assets, stature, etc., but also trade age because he knew that if he were 30 again, he could get to where he is now by the time he reached 40. It was interesting to see the puzzled looks on the young brokers' faces.

One very memorable session I had with Joe was when I was asked to give a talk to our North American managing directors on charitable giving and community involvement. Joe convinced me to title my presentation, "Giving Is Good for Business." He had a spreadsheet brought out that showed his $5,000, $10,000 and $25,000 gives totalling over $2 million per year, and this did not include his major gifts to the United Way, Simon Fraser University, Jewish charities and hospitals. I asked about some of the charities that I had not heard of and he gave to them the amount of their annual budget because he didn't want them wasting money to solicit funds. Just a few months ago, I was involved in the End MS fundraising dinner at the Segals. Joe and Rosalie paid for the dinner and the requirement he placed on us was that we had to raise $400,000 – which all went to charity.

CHAPTER 90

JASON McDOUGALL

CEO/President, FHC Enterprises

I had met Joe a few times when he had come to speak to our local EO chapter. He is always willing, it seems, to help the next generation whenever he can.

As soon as it looked like we might have a real chance at buying Fields, a company that Joe started in 1948, which he later sold to the Bay, I asked a friend of mine if he could help set up a meeting with Joe. Within two days I was in Joe's office talking about this potential deal. Joe was very gracious with his time and offered a few words of wisdom on how to approach the deal, but he was not going to invest, not that day at least. I really wanted him to be part of bringing Fields back into the hands of an entrepreneur and Canadian ownership.

Joe was gracious enough to put up with me for another five meetings until finally he invested what he considered a token investment, which helped us to gather the equity we needed to get the deal done. His head kept saying no and his heart was saying yes. Joe invested on the condition that we would not use his name to raise the balance of the money we needed. We agreed, even though it would have made our lives much easier to raise the balance of the money we needed. We understood.

More than anything, I am thankful to have had the time to see what an amazing person Joe is. He is so real, he readily admits his mistakes and has gained such great wisdom, which he generously shares. He is truly wealthy in every sense of the word. He certainly is someone that I will model much of the rest of my life after.

Thank you, Joe.

CHAPTER 91

ROBERT D. WATT LVO

Chief Herald of Canada (1988-2007)
Rideau Herald Emeritus
Citizenship Judge
Hon. Lieutenant Colonel, 12th Vancouver Field Ambulance

As you would expect, for decades now, Dr. Joe Segal has received many honours, in celebration of his outstanding philanthropy, entrepreneurial leadership and his generous and compassionate nature. He leads by words, deeds and example.

During the time when he served as Chancellor of Simon Fraser University in the early 1990s, when I was working at Rideau Hall in Ottawa, I had the privilege of first getting to know him while he hosted several lunch meetings with me to discuss the design for another national honour, his coat of arms.

The lunches themselves were a delight, and a great learning experience for me, because it was important for me to understand some of the details of his life that Joe considered most important, and wanted to have reflected in his heraldic symbol. Of course, for a man who had already accomplished so much, there were many possible designs that would have served well, to celebrate his extraordinary life.

At the heart of the coat of arms are three ideas: a salute to the four children that he and Rosalie have raised and nurtured; a symbol of his business achievements; and a symbolic recognition of his Jewish heritage. The colours Joe chose also honoured other things that have been central to his life and the many institutions and causes he has championed: his pride in Canada through the national colours of red and white; his ongoing support of Israel and its people, through blue and white; and, to symbolize the wealth he has created through his many business ventures for more than half a century, gold. His two sons and two daughters, who are carrying forward many of his and Rosalie's passions, are represented by four blue maple leaves. Kingswood Capital, the venture capital company he founded in 1979, which has been such a catalyst for so many developments in the region, is at the centre of the shield, in the form of a golden tree, crowned by a circlet of gold Stars of David. I like to think of this element as a special symbol honouring Joe himself who has been like the tree of life to so many; in business, education and health care and in community service in the broadest sense.

Above the shield is a crest, which first honours Rosalie through the roses and which speaks to Joe's Alberta roots, through the same wild rose, to his service to Canada during the Second World War with the Calgary Highlanders Regiment, whose badge shows a beaver. At the time, I thought how apt it was to be able to show a golden beaver, an animal renowned for its industriousness, for a man of industry and determination on an epic scale.

Near the end of one of the lunches I mentioned the need for a motto to complete the symbol. Joe thought a little and then suggested, "Strength and Decisiveness with Compassion." It is hard to imagine, I think, a more perfect summary of his character and approach to life.

In the years since those arms were granted by the Canadian Crown in 1994, as I have continued to enjoy Joe's friendship and lunches where he always showed such interest in how my work was unfolding and was ready with excellent advice on specific issues, he has come to epitomize someone who is indeed strong, decisive and filled with compassion. After each lunch I come away with a renewed appreciation for my good fortune in having our paths cross and having the chance to meet such a wonderful community leader and visionary.

CHAPTER 92

KEN VOTH

President, Voth Bros. Developments Ltd.

I met Joe Segal in December 1989. It was late afternoon when Lorne Segal, my brother Don and I were negotiating a joint venture to build two highrise towers in Surrey's Guildford district. Architectural drawings, pro formas and sales projections covered the table. Then, Joe walked in to the meeting with some Christmas teddy bears. He really knew how to lighten up serious business!

The Segals and the Voths made the deal that day. We built those towers. And I got much more than just an investor (and two teddy bears) from the deal: Joe took me under his wing and we began a relationship that remains integral to my life until this day.

Most of the time when we meet to discuss business, it is over lunch. In the early days, we met at Chartwell; and now we meet at Yew. I look forward to those lunches. Over the years, I have met so many people while out with Joe, as everyone, it seems, wants to say hello to the legendary Joe Segal.

I am always early for lunch to make sure my numbers are right, because Joe is sharp: so sharp that he can call up numbers from projects from 20 years ago. His memory is unbelievable, and he will never let you forget it!

He is consistently interested in how I am doing and is quick to add his advice, which is generous of him and valuable for me.

He has taught me how to reach further and to give more of my time, talent and money to help make the world a better place. Joe and Rosalie have led by example. I have observed them give to the poor, use their voice and leverage their place in society to significantly further causes and organizations they believe in. After attending a dinner at their home one evening, Joe and Rosalie encouraged my wife Betty and me to open our home to causes we believe in. We've taken their advice, and have enjoyed the satisfaction that comes from helping others.

When the economy took a major downturn in 2008, Joe – the guy who lightened up our first meeting by pulling out the teddy bears – encouraged me to *never give up*. That first meeting back in 1989 turned out to be a meeting that most certainly has helped shape who I am today.

As for the teddy bears, I took them home to my two children. Today, more than 20 years later, my four granddaughters still play with them.

Cheers to my good friend, business partner and mentor, to the community builder, to the advocate for the underprivileged . . . Joe Segal.

CHAPTER 93

DAVID R. PODMORE MA (Esc.), D.TECH. (Hon), MCIP, RI, FRI

Chairman & Chief Executive Officer, President & Chief Operating Officer
Concert Properties Ltd.

I have had the extreme good fortune of knowing Joe Segal for over 28 years. I am most grateful for his support in helping Jack Poole and me found Concert Properties in 1989. Through these years I have shared many lunches with Joe, and also enjoyed the warm hospitality of Joe and Rosalie at very special functions in their home.

Any encounter with Joe is uplifting and always focuses at some point on the importance of family and his genuine interest in you.

Every lunch with Joe is an exceptionally positive experience that one leaves wiser, better informed and more confident through Joe's gracious, unselfish sharing of wisdom, insight, relevant experiences and encouragement.

Three examples of Joe's shared wisdom that have positively influenced my career and personal life come to mind.

First, early in my career, Joe imparted an understanding of the importance of a positive forward-looking attitude, encouraging me to "remember the past (but don't dwell on it or past failures), live for the present (embrace, welcome and seize current opportunities) and look to the future (be alert and don't be afraid of new directions)."

Second has been Joe's emphasis on the importance of giving back to our communities, whether through philanthropy, service or both. When I was much younger and my means were less substantial, I remember apologizing to Joe that I could not do more financially to support worthwhile community initiatives. Joe stopped me and said, "Don't ever apologize for this . . . you do something even more difficult . . . you give your time!" These brief words had quite an impact and spurred me to direct even more energy to helping our community through volunteer service.

And third, Joe's encouragement to not waste your "runway." As Joe would advise, each of us has a limited (but unknown) remaining runway in life before our spirit is lifted to the heavens. This is life's most precious asset so we should strive to use it wisely, with purpose and integrity. How each of us chooses to use our remaining runway will differ – for me, again following Joe's example, this means remaining actively engaged as long as physically and mentally able, supporting family, community and country – rejoicing in family achievements, mentoring our youth, giving back through service and philanthropy, remaining gracious under any circumstance, and looking positively and enthusiastically to the future, always conducting oneself with integrity. In short, one would be hard pressed to find a more inspiring mentor and role model than Joe Segal!

CHAPTER 94

MARCEL F. DVORAK MD, FRCSC

Professor of Orthopedics; Head, Division of Spine, University of British Columbia

SUE DVORAK BScPT

We had many times been recipients of the generosity of our friends Rosalie and Joe, being their guests at galas, soirees, concerts and dinner evenings out. We wanted to reciprocate but wondered: what to do for the Segals?

We did what one should do whenever the bar is set too high: we lowered the bar to where it could be stepped over easily. We invited Joe and Rosalie to our lovely but ordinary family home to be served an ordinary family meal, the kind we prepare. They graciously accepted, accompanied by our disclaimer that we call it "supper" in order to lower expectations. Joe's immediate urging was, "Oh, just give me a hot dog!"

The date arrived and we threw the backpacks and dirty soccer cleats downstairs and searched for a couple of spare hangers for the front closet.

The Segals were punctual as usual.

We settled comfortably in the living room while our six children came in and out to be introduced to our guests. Next came the only major faux pas of the evening. The half-decent glasses set out were unfortunately overlooked and instead our cocktails served in appallingly large, dishwasher-etched glass tumblers from Costco. Neither Joe nor Rosalie batted an eyelash, although the ever-attentive Rosalie did send us beautiful glasses the following Christmas.

At dinner, after our soup, we carefully arranged the pièce de résistance beside a linen napkin on a polished silver tray and, with a flourish, Joe Segal was served his hot dog.

We all howled with laughter until tears ran. As I gathered up the tray to fetch the "real supper," Joe stopped me saying, "Hey! I want that hot dog!" That is how it came to pass that Joe Segal sat happily noshing a couple of barbecued all-beef hot dogs while we ate our salmon dinner.

A fabulous evening followed. Settled back in the living room with the kids draped all about, we engaged in lively conversation. Talk meandered to where it always goes with Joe: to love of family, to service, to God, to gratitude, to relationships, to contribution. Joe asked probing questions and elicited thoughtful answers.

Because Joe Segal is a "people person" through and through, intensely interested in what makes people tick, what motivates them, what makes them happy. Joe loves people.

And we love him.

CHAPTER 95

BRIAN HILL

CEO, Aritzia LP

I had only heard of Mr. Segal when I was young and working hard to keep my business afloat. One sunny day, when driving to work, I pulled up next to a distinguished elderly gentleman. Spotless black sedan. Beautiful dark suit contrasting his groomed white hair. Hand on the steering wheel revealing shiny gold cufflinks. He looked over at me, not knowing who I was, and gave me a warm accepting smile . . . I knew immediately who was driving the car.

Years later, I found myself sitting across from Mr. Segal over lunch. Mentor, business partner and friend.

The mentor, excited to discuss anything retail. Informing me how he recently analyzed my company's operations from outside our store adjacent to his office lobby. Dissecting our company's financial results with precision accuracy, explaining the finer details of what I previously thought was a complicated business. Astonishing, considering he had never seen our company's financial statements.

The business partner explaining to me how important it is not to be greedy. That loyalty is important. Always ensuring, whenever possible, that everyone wins. Not to ever worry about the crumbs.

The friend, explaining to me that no matter how important

business is, family and friends are more important. To be a leader in the community. How to give back and why it is so important.

I look forward to every one of our lunches, feeling fortunate that a few times a year, I am the privileged one announcing to the host at the Four Seasons: "I'm having lunch with Mr. Segal today."

CHAPTER 96

DARCY REZAC

CEO, Anapacific Consulting

GAYLE HALLGREN-REZAC

Shepa Learning Company

Joe is a successful businessman, he's rich – probably not the richest guy in town, monetarily – but he is one rich guy where it really counts. He's rich in friends, rich in wisdom and rich in family. But the story of Joe wouldn't be complete without the story of Rosalie. Here is what makes them really special. Joe and Rosalie could easily live their life among a select group of friends. They've done the heavy lifting in life and they can afford to just sit back and relax. But that is not what they do. Instead, they show up for benefits, Joe always is the first to make the donation, and he's also there to 'top up' the amount when others sit on their hands. And, they open their palatial home to myriad good causes. They host the event (translation: they pay for a fabulous Four Seasons catered dinner, Rosalie organizes all the details, and then they are the gracious hosts for the evening).

You know Joe would be just as happy kicking back with an excellent Cuban cigar and a single malt and Rosalie has done her fair share of table seating charts and 'hostess with the mostess' duties. But they are members of what Robert Putnam, author of the seminal book on social capital, *Bowling Alone*, calls the "long civic generation," those individuals born in the first third of the 20th century who understand the value of participating and contributing to the social capital of society.

In 2012, Joe spoke at an event honouring his son Lorne, for the work Lorne has done with the Courage to Come Back Awards and his hands-on labour of love with We Day. Joe began his remarks by noting that Lorne and his team, including his wife Melita, put a huge amount of personal effort into these two causes: "I tell Lorne, just write the cheque." He got the laugh. But that was the mischievous Joe, because what Joe's family has learned is it's not just about being a contributor, it's about being a participant as well.

This hands-on approach has given Joe great empathy and he connects with people in an amazing way. Recently we bumped into Joe on his way back from lunch at Yew in the Four Seasons, as he was walking through the Pacific Centre Mall. We introduced him to two filmmakers who are working on a project to raise awareness of how, as individuals and as groups, we can create social change. We had just spent an hour talking about the concept, trying to capture the essence, and then we met Joe. Joe immediately understood what filmmakers Jon and Laura were doing. He said, "If you do it well, you have the opportunity to soften hearts." Exactly.

CHAPTER 97

BLAYNE JOHNSON

Chairman, Featherstone Capital

Many years ago as a young man, I found myself in quite a pickle. The business I had started as a student in business school at Simon Fraser University had gone bust and I was looking for a new career. The best idea I could come up with at the time was to write a letter to Joe Segal, whom I had met as a student representative on the board of governors of SFU a few years earlier, asking for some of his time and advice. I enclosed a crisp new $50 bill demonstrating that I was willing to pay for his time.

Joe kindly let me spend the day in his office explaining between his many meetings and business dealings, how to build my own fortune and meaningful life. Start in sales – stock market or real estate – save my capital, invest it wisely, stay late and work weekends so that I could learn how to do my own deals. Sow before I reaped, be of service, treat others with an even hand, all the while keeping family front and centre in life. If I stayed the course, eventually my capital would be working so well that I would not have to.

Incredibly, that dream turned into my reality. Joe continued to meet with me over the years offering advice and encouragement. This was an extraordinary thing for a man, who had just been profiled in Peter C. Newman's book *The Acquisitors* as one of Canada's foremost businessmen, to do. Extending a helping hand to a lost young "want-to-be businessman" from the prairies – but that is the true essence of Joe Segal.

When you are as good at something and as successful as Joe, it is easy to intimidate or make people feel small with your greatness. In Joe's case, he shares his experience, knowledge and expertise in a way that invites us into his joy – the delight of doing business in a clever, morally correct, ethical manner and in doing so makes us feel more powerful. He lights up engaging you in a way that connects us to our own joyfulness – to believe that we too can do something truly extraordinary. I will be forever grateful for the sage advice, encouragement and words of wisdom, but most of all for the love behind all of that. Only a truly wonderful human being is able to share himself in that way.

CHAPTER 98

LYALL KNOTT Q.C.

Partner, Clark Wilson LLP

It is true that there are few people who have lunch with Joe as often as I do . . . albeit at separate tables.

Since I was first called to the Bar in 1974, I have always worked within walking distance of the Four Seasons Hotel. Early on in my career I got into the habit of lunching at the fine-dining restaurant in the Four Seasons, Chartwell. There in the corner sat Joe Segal presiding over the restaurant. Indeed, the Four Seasons honoured him by placing a painting of the Churchillian Residence of Chartwell, behind Joe's table.

Over time we became accustomed to seeing each other across the restaurant and so when Chartwell closed, we both took our patronage across the hotel lobby to the new Yew Restaurant.

Day after day we see each other at lunch and over time a friendship has evolved not only with Joe, but also with his sons Lorne and Gary. Joe has mentored me and he has taught me some of the great pleasures in life, including a dry martini made with Hendrick's gin.

Best known in our community for his business acumen, community involvement and generous support of community organizations, Joe's greatest pride is his family. He has been appropriately recognized with many honours including the Order of British Columbia and the Order of Canada. Joe and Rosalie are true leaders of our community.

What isn't well known about Joe is his wartime service as a soldier with the Calgary Highlanders.

His is a story of a young, patriotic Canadian who volunteered in the Second World War to serve and to "Stand on Guard" for Canada.

Military service is like no other community service. Joe was prepared to put his life on the line to defend his country.

As the Honourary Captain, Canadian Fleet Pacific, Royal Canadian Navy, I have had the occasion to invite Joe to speak to young Canadian veterans returning home from the battlefields of Afghanistan. Joe spoke to these young Canadian men and women as a colleague. He told the story of his attempt to enlist in the Navy but somehow found himself as a Private with the Calgary Highlanders. It was off to boot camp, followed by deployment to the European theatre where he served with distinction. Joe talked openly about being a frightened, lonely young man facing a hostile enemy far from home. Joe's message inspired those young Canadians who, like Joe, stood in harm's way to protect the Canadian way of life.

Upon the cessation of hostilities, Sergeant Segal was honourably discharged from the Canadian Army and returned home to make his life and career in a peaceful Canada.

Like so many Canadians of his generation, Sergeant Joe Segal of the Calgary Highlanders is a Canadian hero.

CHAPTER 99

HERBERT MICHAEL EVERS

President, Waterstone Properties

I first met Joe Segal 30 years ago through the local business magazines and newspapers and their articles on this successful businessman who was turning the Canadian retail industry on its ear. I was a freshly graduated business student and had no idea I would have lunch with Joe 20 years later and help run one of his companies for the past 17 years.

First National Properties was the successor to Block Bros. and a company acquired by Joe Segal and his partners in 1988. Jim Winton was president of the company and became a good friend through our association at the Vancouver Lawn Tennis & Badminton Club. In 1995, Jim asked me to come work at First National and I jumped at the opportunity. Unfortunately, Jim's life was cut short by pancreatic cancer, and six months after starting I was asked if I would manage the company and report to the board, which consisted of Joe Segal, Arthur Block, Milan Ilich, Morley Koffman and Leon Kahn. It was a wonderful opportunity and I was scared out of my mind.

I will never forget my first First National board meeting, which was held in the offices of Koffman Kalef. Everyone sat in a designated seat, with Joe in the Chair. To say I was intimidated by the business acumen in the room would be a gross understatement. Joe made it abundantly clear from the start that he appreciated my opinion and expected me to speak my mind regarding the business plan First National was pursuing. Joe has an uncanny ability to look through the negative aspect of any deal and to see clearly why a property should be developed or a building bought or sold. I quickly saw firsthand Joe's legendary analytical skills and his ability to dissect numbers.

After a number of years, I also learned that Joe had a tendency to use a number of scenarios that he knew backwards and forwards in all forms of measure. Whether it be value per front foot, per square foot, per buildable foot or any other metric, Joe had his scenarios for every form of real estate. This skill allowed Joe to challenge any proposal put in front of him and ensured the presenter was thoroughly committed to his recommendation and had done his homework. Today I think of Joe and his questions every time I think I know something about real estate and I ask myself, do I really know what I'm talking about or would Segal see right through me?

Joe is a tremendous mentor and a partner who never wavers in his support. Joe is never afraid to make a decision and always trusts his instincts. I heard one friend say to Joe that he was "too old to buy green bananas." Joe's reaction was swift and he said that once you feel you're too old to do anything, you might as well put one foot in the grave. Real estate success does not happen overnight and Joe recognized you have to take advantage of opportunities when they are presented and treat every day the same. I am certain that regardless of age, Joe will always remain forever young.

In terms of Joe's generosity and philanthropy, the examples are countless. I will never forget one occasion at the Four Seasons when Joe asked, in typical fashion, "What's new?" I told him about my work in soccer and how we were trying to generate some support for one of the schools from the Vancouver East Side. After listening for a few minutes, Joe pulled out his wallet, looked at me and said, "How much are you giving? I'll match it." That type of spontaneous generosity is representative of his continual support of our community and those who are less fortunate. Although Joe and Rosalie have been major benefactors in our city, it is often not the size of the donation that matters, but the philosophy to give back what you can to make our world a little better. More than anything else, that will be Joe Segal's legacy.

CHAPTER 100

R.J. (BOB) STEWART LL.D. (Hon)

Chief Constable (Rtd.), Vancouver Police Department

Joe Segal, now that's a name that is hard to forget.

My personal knowledge of Joe's community involvement covers many years and a wide spectrum of activity. As a native Vancouverite and having been involved in the public scene for most of my life, I have had ample opportunity to personally witness or be privy to the unending good works performed by Joe and his good wife Rosalie.

One example involves the early days of the Vancouver Police Foundation when the task was to bring together a group of high-profile Vancouver businessmen, entrepreneurs and community-minded citizens. Joe met all of those criteria and joined in this worthwhile initiative thereby greatly assisting the Foundation to establish a place in the community. From the early 1980s to 2008, Joe was a leading member of this dedicated group ensuring that the Foundation would become an effective body providing much-needed funding and support for Police Department research and specialized equipment not normally available through regular channels. Joe's success in business is well known and needs no further comment.

Joe and Rosalie's commitment to community deserves a

special acknowledgement. This wonderful couple is present whenever there is a call to sponsor, contribute to and to attend many of Vancouver's charitable and civic fundraising events. A legacy has been well established and it continues to grow.

Joe's personal commitment to an exhaustive list of charities regardless of the cause is unprecedented in this city. The Segal name is attached to dozens of public and private awards of recognition. Recognition has often reached beyond the local scene with numerous national and international tributes adding to the very long and outstanding list of accomplishments.

I have been very fortunate in my capacity as a citizen, a former Vancouver Police Chief and an officer of Variety International – The Children's Charity, to have worked with and shared special time with Joe and Rosalie over many years. Vancouver is a better place because of their outstanding commitment to community.

CHAPTER 101

MICHAEL AUDAIN O.C., O.B.C.

Chairman, Polygon Homes Ltd.

Since British Columbia's early days, there have been men who have risen to positions of prominence and influence, not by birth into an aristocratic or moneyed family, but by their own brilliance and sheer hard work. Such a man is Joe Segal.

Joe's record of accomplishment in the business world can be told by others. Suffice it to say that in the second half of the 20th century, he has had few peers.

But, what is especially remarkable is that Joe and Rosalie have used their wealth not to acquire symbols of wealth and affluence, such as a corporate jet, a private yacht a block in length, or an art collection that rivals the Medicis'. Rather, they have put their financial resources at the service of the community in which they have contributed magnificently to numerous causes, but most notably in health and education.

I have not been a partner or confidant of Joe's. In fact, I can only recall a single lunch at his hallowed Four Seasons table, but over the years I have had the good fortune to come to know Joe and his family well enough that I can sense how genuine their care for our community has been.

And that time I lunched with Joe? Well, it was about a deal that

I was proposing to partner with him. But, Joe's probing questions caused me to rethink the deal to the point that I didn't proceed with it. As Joe said later, "Well, Michael, often the best deal is the one you don't do." And he was undoubtedly right.

What's also so interesting about Joe is that he is a superstar Canadian business executive who, like his friend Jimmy Pattison, never thought it necessary to move to Toronto. This surely illustrates that we can do big things by remaining resident out here in God's country on the West Coast.

It is a privilege to salute Joe on all his remarkable accomplishments. What an example his record of achievement in business and philanthropy will be for British Columbians in the decades to come!

CHAPTER 102

DON LINDSAY

President & CEO, Teck Resources Limited

I remember very clearly when I first met Joe Segal. In the spring of 2005 I left my job in Toronto as president of CIBC World Markets and moved to Vancouver as the incoming CEO of Teck Resources. The setting of our meeting was the home of Joe and Rosalie Segal; they hosted a reception and dinner to raise awareness of the good work performed by the heart health-care unit of Vancouver General Hospital. Feeling very much the newcomer among the 90 or 100 people in attendance, I was so touched by Joe and Rosalie's efforts to welcome me and make me feel comfortable.

That night I was there to announce that Teck would make a gift of $1 million to help buy a key piece of equipment, as well as to announce that Teck would match any further gifts from our employees. It was the beginning of a dramatic change in Teck's community investment approach. Now that I have lived in B.C. for over eight years, it seems fitting that it began in the garden of Joe Segal, a man who indisputably is one of the real leaders in giving back to the community.

Throughout the years, Joe has been incredibly gracious whenever I have seen him. One occasion stands out in my mind, the night Joe and Rosalie hosted an event for B.C. Children's Hospital.

As chair of the Campaign for B.C. Children, I truly appreciated their hospitality because it was very helpful to our donor cultivation efforts. But more than that, I enjoyed the evening because they are such kind hosts; they exude the civility of a time gone by.

I remember talking to Joe about his tenure with the board of the Hudson's Bay Company. Years before, I had been the lead banker for Sears and worked towards a nationwide swap of store locations and real estate assets between Sears and Hudson's Bay. When Joe heard about my involvement, he immediately went downstairs to retrieve a very special bottle of cognac that I believe was part of a case given to him when he retired. It had an authentic and historic Hudson's Bay Company label on it and was clearly a valuable collectors' bottle. But Joe wanted someone to have it who would understand how special it was and the traditions it represented. And, if you are wondering, I still have not finished the bottle because I treasure every ounce, not so much because it is a rare and historic cognac, but because of the man it came from.

I see Joe several times a year and most of the time it is at events where either he or now his sons, Lorne and Gary, are playing a leading role in helping out a lot of people. It is a real tribute that Joe has been able to pass on such a generous spirit to the next generation of his family. That in itself is a great testament to the character of the man. I think of Joe as a wonderful example of a very decent human being and a role model for all of us.

CHAPTER 103

PETER H. THOMAS LL.D. (Hon)

Chairman & CEO, Thomas Franchise Solutions Ltd.

When asked to describe my 25-plus-year friendship with the renowned entrepreneur Joe Segal, my brain flooded with wonderful memories. Joe has been a friend and a mentor to me and an inspiration behind my own values-based leadership journey.

I'm often asked to name the three outstanding qualities of people I respect. With Joe, I feel compelled to double my answer. Here are the top six reasons why, to me, Joe truly is an exceptional leader.

Honesty: Joe says what he means and does what he believes to be right at all times. He is true to his word and his response is always pure . . . from the heart and based on his vast experience as an entrepreneur and philanthropist.

Charm: Joe has the unique ability to make you feel special. When you speak to him you quickly realize he is listening to every word with complete focus and undivided attention.

Cool: It's not just his great ties or his ability to keep up with the latest trends. Cool is also Joe's demeanour. He is forever the statesman and a man of many accomplishments.

Wisdom: Talking to Joe is always a learning opportunity. It's not just what he says, but how he says it. Being ever so humble, he doesn't see himself as a wise man but simply shares his endless knowledge and experience to help others.

Charitable: Joe is the kind of philanthropist that not only gives but inspires others to do the same. Watching him raise and contribute money to various charities over the years motivated me to make charity a large part of my life.

Optimism: Many fortunes were made and lost over the years I've known Joe, and not once did I hear him complain. To Joe, there is always a bright side to look forward to and another opportunity right around the corner.

Cheers to Joe and his infectious spirit and limitless generosity. The world became a better place the day he was born. I feel blessed to have him in my life.

CHAPTER 104

MICHAEL GELLER AIBC, FCIP, RPP

President, The Geller Group

I will never forget my first dealings with Joe Segal. I had arranged to purchase a site at West 5th and Highbury in Point Grey and Lorne saw a model of the proposed building in my boardroom. "What's this?" he asked. When I explained the situation he said it might be something he and his dad could be interested in.

Lorne arranged for me to meet Joe on Friday afternoon. Unfortunately, something came up and I was asked to come by the house on Sunday. At the time, Joe lived in the magnificent Rio Vista on Southwest Marine Drive. Driving through the ornate gates in my five-year-old Jag, I was soon surrounded by the Segal fleet of shiny new British cars. I remember feeling quite intimidated.

After Lorne gave me a tour of the house, we went into an elegant den where Joe was seated in a leather chair. I handed him my project pro forma and personal financial statement. Joe scanned the papers quickly and then looked up at me. In a fatherly voice he said, "Michael, the deal looks good. You're a well-regarded guy. But how come you don't have any money?"

All I could say was, "Joe, until now I never really needed any!"

Kingswood Properties was born and our project 2020 Highbury went smoothly. Joe and Lorne were great partners. One day, a realtor brought us an offer from someone who wanted to buy the whole building. I hesitated until Joe turned to me and said, "Michael, we're selling. You'll never go broke taking a profit!"

A decade later we got to collaborate again; this time at SFU. Joe had recently stepped down as Chancellor and I was the newly appointed president of the university's Development Corporation. One day I needed help with the project financing. I called Joe and he invited me to lunch at Chartwell. After a delightful meal, he asked to see the bank's proposal. He then went through it line by line, instructing me on which terms to accept and which to negotiate. After he finished, I thanked him profusely and I remember him saying, "Now under no circumstances must HSBC know I helped you with this."

Joe, over your many decades you have helped a lot of people without others knowing. Thank you. May you live to 120!

CHAPTER 105

AVTAR BAINS

President, Premise Properties

It was a lovely evening in Vancouver, in the spring of 1998, when Joe and Rosalie Segal joined my wife Monika and me at our home for dinner.

A perfect night for a dry martini, good food, wonderful conversation and indeed, it was a night to learn.

First and foremost on Joe's mind was the wellbeing of our family. This is always the starting point for the Segals, whether or not business is the explicit focal point. Their concern for the welfare of my wife and children is at the forefront of their mindset, and this is an unwavering trait of the family.

A discussion surrounding the Segal family served as a segue to learn about their progress, including a conversation about their grandson, Danny Miller, whom I had the opportunity to coach in youth soccer in the 1980s. Before long, the discussion turned to business "war stories" and we were thoroughly entertained while listening to Joe's anecdotes, with topics ranging from the acquisition of Zellers, to various real estate deals and the intricacies of operating businesses. Over the course of the evening, one thing became abundantly clear; and that was the theme of balance. Balance of family, friends, business, the community and caring for others.

Joe went on to explain that it is not possible to individually or collectively achieve true success in any one of these aspects of life, without producing collateral good in each of the others. It is a quid pro quo scenario – contributing to the community and caring for others is also good for our family. Joe recently exemplified this concept with his contribution to the VGH & UBC Hospital Foundation, supporting mental health by way of the construction of a new facility. This is just one of many examples of Mr. Segal's incredible community initiatives, benefiting innumerable B.C. residents.

It is this "go forward" mentality, consideration of balance, and spirit of generosity that keeps both British Columbia and Canada as a model for the rest of the world.

What one ultimately realizes is that for Mr. Joseph Segal, there is no distinction between the opportunity to help others and the opportunity to grow one's self. In Mr. Segal's own words: "It is all about seeing opportunity where others do not."

CHAPTER 106

JOHN C. KERR C.M., O.B.C., LL.D.

Chairman, Lignum Investments Ltd.

I have been having lunch with Joe since the early days at Chartwell. Back then I was a young businessman trying to stay alive in the lumber business, which was no small trick. Even though Joe had no connection to my business, he was a great listener and inevitably understood my problems, which over the years ranged from having no money to having to deal with U.S. trade problems. He always seemed to know which question to ask and to know the answer before I gave it. His combination of down-home analysis and toughness tempered with optimism was formidable. Over the years, Joe's advice has always been rock solid; I just wish I had followed more of it. Whether it was retail or real estate, Joe had an unerring ability to cut through the nonsense and get to the point. Joe always knew how to say no. He was the only person who could turn me down entirely and leave me feeling good about it. No matter how bleak the situation, Joe has always been able to find the silver lining and always has an idea about what to do next. Finally, Joe has a fabulous taste both in fashion and more importantly in women. They don't come any better than Rosalie. He is always on my good side because he loves my wife Judy almost as much as I do.

All in all, one of a kind!

ABOUT THE AUTHOR

PETER LEGGE, O.B.C. • LL.D. (Hon) • D.Tech. • CSP • CPAE • HoF

Peter Legge is an inspiration to anyone who meets him. He lives his life's dream as an internationally acclaimed professional speaker, bestselling author and as Chairman and CEO of the largest, independently owned magazine publishing company in Western Canada – Canada Wide Media Limited. Peter is a community leader who tirelessly devotes his time to many worthwhile organizations and was recently named one of the 2012 top 25 immigrant entrepreneurs in Canada.

His presentations are based on his everyday experiences as a community leader, husband, father and CEO. Peter has published 16 previous books, his most recent being the sixth volume of his bestselling series, *If Only I'd Said That.* His books have motivated thousands of people towards positive change.

Toastmasters International has voted Peter "Golden Gavel Award Winner" and "Top Speaker in North America," and both the National Speakers Association and the Canadian Association of Professional Speakers have inducted him into the Speakers Hall of Fame.

Peter is also a member of the prestigious Speakers Roundtable, an invitation-only society comprising 20 of North America's top professional speakers. He is the recipient of three honorary doctorate degrees, and in 2006, the Peter Legge Philanthropist of the Year Award was introduced by the Canadian Association of Professional Speakers. Peter was the first recipient of this award.

In June 2008, the province's highest honour, the Order of British Columbia, was presented to Peter for his lifelong commitment to serving the community.

In the summer of 2012, Peter was honoured by Douglas College with the establishment of the Peter Legge International Institute of Sales Excellence. Later the same year, he was one of a number of recipients presented with the Queen's Diamond Jubilee Medal in honour of his significant achievements and contributions to British Columbia.

To contact Peter, write to:

Peter Legge Management Company Ltd.
4180 Lougheed Hwy, 4th Floor
Burnaby, BC V5C 6A7 Canada
Telephone: 604-299-7311
Email: plegge@canadawide.com
Website: www.peterlegge.com

To order Peter's books, CDs and other products,
please visit *www.peterlegge.com*
or email Heidi Christie at hchristie@canadawide.com